Dr. Nicole B. Simpson & Sonji K. Grandy
Present

A Legacy of Light

Creating Legacy Through Service

Generation X Collective

THIS IS A WRITTEN WORK BY
NICOLE B. SIMPSON, SONJI K. GRANDY & THE GENERATION X COLLECTIVE
PUBLISHED BY HarvestWealth Publishing

This book is based on the divinely inspired thoughts and life experiences of **Nicole B. Simpson, Sonji K. Grandy & The Generation X Collective**.

All content therein is written as recalled and recounted by them.
All identities are used by permission or purposely omitted to protect the privacy of those living or dead.

A LEGACY OF LIGHT

By Nicole B. Simpson, Sonji K. Grandy & The Generation X Collective

Published in the United States of America by
Nicole B. Simpson & Sonji K. Grandy
An imprint of HarvestWealth Publishing

www.GenerationXCommunity.com

Library of Congress Cataloguing-In-Publication Number **PENDING**

ISBN 979-8-9871782-9-4
First Edition Printing
Printed in the United States of America
March 2026

DEDICATION

This book is dedicated to the people who were never meant to be invisible—
the children whose names were called when systems fell silent,
the families standing in the narrow space between survival and stability,
and the voices that refused to be muted when justice demanded sound.

It is dedicated to every young person who was invited not just to watch,
but to participate—to learn, to lead, to imagine themselves differently
because someone believed access was a right, not a reward.

It is dedicated to those who carried dignity into rooms where it was often absent,
who served without shame, who gave without condition,
and who understood that true community work begins with respect.

It is dedicated to returning citizens reclaiming purpose,
to incarcerated men and women seen not as statistics,
but as human beings worthy of restoration, opportunity, and hope.

It is dedicated to the faithful servants—board members, mentors, volunteers,
leaders, and partners—who governed with integrity,
stood firm through change, and remained rooted when the work was hard and the road was long.

Above all, this book is dedicated to the belief that faith in action matters,
that no child should ever be left behind,
and that when people stand in the gap for one another,
entire communities can change.

This is for the lives restored,
the futures reclaimed,
and the dignity preserved—

ACKNOWLEDGEMENTS

We proudly acknowledge Jesse L. Simpson III and Sherri Hedgeman as founding members of the Generation X Community Association. Your vision, commitment, and willingness to build from the ground up laid a foundation that continues to impact lives and communities in meaningful and lasting ways.

With deep gratitude, we extend our appreciation to Rev. Dr. Lewis J. Dixon, Richard Anderson, Rev. Dr. Crystal R. White, Apostle Gwendolyn Carson, and Elder Stephanie Knight for their willingness to enter correctional facilities throughout the state of New Jersey to serve. Your courage, compassion, and commitment to showing up behind the walls brought hope, spiritual support, and dignity to those often forgotten and strengthened the mission of the Generation X Community Association through faithful presence and hands-on service.

We also acknowledge the Edna Mahan Correctional Facility, with special thanks to Miss Jane Pursell, the employee who opened the door for the Generation X Community Association to engage in prison ministry. Your willingness to trust the vision made it possible for transformation, healing, and restoration to reach those who needed it most. We are equally grateful for the partnership of the Focus on the Victim Program, whose collaboration and shared commitment to advocacy and restoration amplified this work.

To every individual who, while incarcerated, took the time to join The Power of Gospel and the Generation X Community Association in service and programming—we honor you. Your participation, resilience, and willingness to grow and give back stand as powerful testimony to purpose, redemption, and hope.

We gratefully acknowledge the New Jersey Department of Corrections for supporting the Dare 2 Dream Institute with financial resources that helped expand the reach and effectiveness of this work. Your support affirmed the value of empowerment, education, and second chances.

Finally, we extend our heartfelt gratitude to Dr. DeLacy D. Davis. Without your timely pep talk and encouragement, we would never have walked through the open door that led to this level of service. Your words sparked action, and that action continues to bear fruit.

We close by honoring our families, whose unwavering support sustained us throughout this journey, the prayers and covering of Micah 7 Ministries, and our publishing partner, The Legna Agency, whose belief in the vision helped bring this work to life.

With sincere appreciation,
Nicole and Sonji

TABLE OF CONTENTS

THE FIRST BRICK

From Complaint to Commitment

Sonji K. Grandy

Every legacy begins with a moment that is usually quiet, often unplanned, but always charged with purpose.

Ours began in my apartment in Bayonne, New Jersey, in the summer of 2000.

It wasn't a boardroom. There were no bylaws, no funding, no five-year plan. Just four people who loved their city deeply and were fed up with watching it fall apart from a distance. That evening, my sister **Nicole B. Simpson**, not yet *Dr. Simpson*, my best friend **Sherri Hedgeman**, **Jesse L. Simpson III**, and I gathered the way we always did: to laugh, decompress, and share space. It was customary for us. Safe. Familiar.

But that night, the conversation shifted.

At the time, I was transitioning out of my role at a nonprofit health center, having worked on the front lines of community care. I had seen the gaps up close, the people who fell through them, and the systems that quietly failed them. All of us, though no longer living in Jersey City, were still deeply connected through family, friendships, and our work. And what we were seeing disturbed us.

The potholes were wrecking our cars, the children were being overlooked, resources were thin, and hope felt even thinner, everyday reminders that the systems meant to serve the community were failing the very people who depended on them most.

So we made a decision that night, not a casual one, but a deliberate commitment that would change the course of our lives and our community.

We understood that if we were going to talk about change, we had to be willing to *create* it. Complaints without action were no longer acceptable. Awareness without accountability was not enough. What was required was courage, the kind that moves before everything is perfectly in place.

At the time, Jersey City was at a crossroads. The city was navigating a major political shift, with the possibility of electing its first African American mayor, while still grappling with long-standing inequities that had gone unaddressed for decades. Neighborhoods were changing unevenly, economic development was visible in some areas and nonexistent in others, and many residents, especially children and working families, were being left behind in the transition. It was a moment filled with both hope and tension, and we felt an undeniable responsibility to be part of what came next.

Our first step was bold, especially for a group with no official name, no nonprofit status, and no guarantee of being taken seriously. Yet we moved anyway. We decided to seek out the mayoral candidates and introduce ourselves as a new organization, not as a future idea, but as a present force. Not someday, when the paperwork was complete or the funding secured. Now.

The Simpson family's media show became an unexpected but powerful doorway. It gave us access to many grassroots organizations that never received it, and we understood the responsibility that came with that privilege. We used the platform with intention and integrity, conducting fair and impartial interviews that centered the real concerns of real people, questions rooted in infrastructure, education, safety, and opportunity. We listened closely to the answers, not as spectators, but as community members invested in the outcome.

That moment taught us something foundational: when purpose meets opportunity, movement begins. We did not yet know what Generation X Community Association would become, but we knew who we were called to be engaged, informed, and unafraid to step into spaces where our voices were needed. Acting in that historical moment, before we were fully ready, became the first brick laid in a legacy that continues to serve, advocate, and stand in the gap to this day.

That's when we saw it, the power of media as a tool for accountability, education, and exposure.

That spark became a blueprint. What started as civic engagement quickly evolved into something larger. We leaned into mentorship and internships, particularly in music and television. Young people found their way to us, curious, creative, searching. By the time of Generation X, they were no longer spectators; they became participants. They learned the language of media, the discipline of production, and the importance of having a voice.

As they grew, so did we. When internships ended, we didn't want the opportunity to stop there. So we expanded, introducing scholarships to support college and trade school dreams. Over time, the scholarships grew in size and scope. Banquets followed. Then presentations. We made space to honor students not just for grades, but for effort, service, and heart.

We dared to be different. We opened our doors to students already in school and to those who weren't "A students." We believed community involvement mattered just as much as academic performance because service hood was the very foundation of Generation X Community Association. Before we ever had formal programs, we had values.

One of our earliest lessons came during the holidays. Our first toy giveaway was small, hosted in a hair salon in Jersey City. We didn't have many toys. The quality, if I'm honest, was subpar. We weren't sure who would come, or if anyone would come at all.

But the line wrapped around the corner. Some families waited patiently. Some were grateful. Others were not.

That moment humbled us and taught us something critical: **the need was far greater than we imagined**. It shaped how we showed up moving forward. Today, our annual toy giveaways are anticipated as early as September. We partner across the State of New Jersey, fundraise independently, and maintain one unwavering principle:

No child gets left behind.

Our focus has always been the overlooked middle, the families just above the poverty line and just below stability, living in a space that statistics rarely capture, and policies often ignore. They earn just enough to be disqualified from assistance, yet never enough to feel secure. Too "well-off" for help, too stretched to survive, they carry the quiet burden of making impossible choices every day. Society assumes they're fine because they are functioning, because the lights are still on and the doors are still locked at night. But we knew better, because we were them.

We understood the pressure of holding everything together with no safety net. We knew what it meant to work hard and still fall short, to navigate systems designed to overlook people who don't fit neatly into categories of need. That lived experience shaped our compassion and sharpened our resolve. We weren't interested in symbolic gestures or surface-level solutions; we wanted to meet people where they actually lived, in the tension between pride and desperation, dignity and need.

So, we chose to stand in the gap.

Standing in the gap meant acknowledging a reality others preferred to ignore and committing to serve without judgment or excessive restriction. It meant offering support before the crisis turned into a collapse. It meant seeing value in families and individuals long before labels or circumstances defined them. That posture of service was not theoretical; it was deeply personal.

That desire to serve people like us, people who just needed someone to see them, to validate their struggle without shaming, is what fueled that conversation more than twenty-five years ago in my living room. It is the same desire that continues to guide Generation X Community Association today, reminding us that the most powerful work often happens not at the extremes, but in the quiet spaces where people are doing their best and still need someone willing to stand beside them.

In 2001, we made it official. We became a nonprofit and named ourselves **Generation X Community Association** because that's who we were. Gen Xers. Builders. Bridge-makers. Change agents who refused to wait for permission.

Over the past 25 years, board members have come and gone, programs have evolved, and our reach has expanded, but the foundation has never shifted. Every person who has served this organization has contributed to its legacy.

This anthology reflects that truth.

The stories that follow, told by returning citizens who have walked through the Dare 2 Dream Institute, are proof that community investment changes lives. Their success is our success. Their freedom, purpose, and transformation are the continuation of a promise we made long ago:

To stop complaining.
To start building.
And to never abandon our people.

GENERATION
X

WHAT BROKE ME BUILT THE WORK

Legacy Through Service

Dr. Nicole B. Simpson

Legacy is not simply what one leaves behind in material terms, but the impact and values woven into the fabric of a community through acts of service, compassion, and a commitment to uplifting others. It is the enduring influence of efforts to preserve dignity, address unmet needs, and inspire future generations to continue the work of positive change.

If we were being honest, I don't think anyone is thinking about legacy until they begin to mature. However, one can encounter something drastic and life-altering, and then begin to ask themselves, "Why am I here?" or "What is my purpose?" or even "How will people remember me when I am gone?" I'm no different. Over 25 years ago, I was at my sister's house with my then-husband, Jeseman, and her friend, Sherri. I cannot remember the details, and recall with specificity is not my thing. I can butcher the recall of a moment in a heartbeat. What I do remember is our frustration with Jersey City's lack of responsiveness to the community's needs. After complaining tirelessly, we decided to put our money where our mouths were and do something. We had the advantage of understanding we could use the media to help us in our quest, so we decided to get involved in the first mayoral race with a black candidate by the name of Glenn Cunningham.

The concept was simple. We were going to represent the people. We offered every candidate an opportunity to present their case for why they should be elected for all the local elections. The people running for city council were given 10 minutes to earn their constituents' votes, while those running for mayor were given 30 minutes. We invited them to our television studio, which was not even in Jersey City, but they came. Free media time to a collective audience was like having prime real estate at the peak of a housing market. I was a television personality at the origin of the hip-hop generation, and Jeseman was politically connected through his association with the local cable news station, so we knew we had something valuable to offer.

We compiled the questions from our viewers, and that is how the Generation X Community Association was established. Upon reflection, we burst on the scene, and it was so impactful that we continued to test the waters of serving through a toy giveaway thereafter. I'm not sure how the rest of the team would define it, but I will say this. The experience was powerful enough for us to continue to press forward, yet humbling enough to recognize that even if you have the desire to serve, delivery matters.

I think it's fair to say the organization was in operation for nearly a year before we officially formulated Generation X Community Association in April 2001. Sonji has focused on our organizational backdrop, but even as I am writing today, I have been struggling with the reality that I definitely hijacked the original vision. I can tell you we were frustrated. I know we came to the realization that if we wanted to see change, we had to get involved. I know we were concerned about the next generation of youth. We were parents of young children, and we didn't like the direction we saw the community going in. That was the original vision. Then, on September 11, 2001, it happened.

I was directly impacted by the tragedy of September 11th, 2001, and I needed help. I was 30 years old, a wife and mother with 2 children. I had a wonderful career, and I was just beginning to build my life. I had moved out of Jersey City, but was still committed to serving the community I had grown up in. I quickly realized that I was drowning financially because I was in a commission-based business. Life is great when you are earning over $100,000 a year. Yet business dried up rapidly, and I had no direction. It was several colleagues who did not look like me who recommended I seek out the support of local agencies. September 11th was so devastating for the entire country that the impact on the financial mecca caused people to give generously. Nonprofit organizations were collecting millions from people across the world to help people like me, or so I thought. As I began to seek help from the likes of the Salvation Army and Red Cross, I experienced great humiliation. The level of disrespect levied against me broke me. I made up in my mind that I would help people and I would not strip their dignity in the process. Never kick someone while they are at their lowest, especially if you have been called to serve.

Research shows that the Salvation Army was among the organizations that arrived on the scene on September 11th within the first hour of the tragedy. They offered food assistance, spiritual counseling, and financial support to first responders, the families of victims and survivors. I was identified as a survivor. Significant resources were poured into the organization. The American Red Cross launched the Liberty Fund and raised over 500 million for what was supposed to be victim assistance. I am prayerful that my personal experience does not reflect how they engage with victims day to day, but it was my story, and it shaped my life.

Initially, I was so grateful to be alive that I never considered seeking assistance. However, after almost a month, several colleagues continued to share how helpful the organizations were and how they would not be able to survive financially during such a dark time. By vocation, I work in a predominantly white male service industry. I entered the securities industry in 1991. I earned my Series 7 in 1992 and began to work my way up so that by September of 2001, I had also acquired my Series 63, 65, my life and health designation along with my CFP® designation. I worked at Morgan Stanley as a financial advisor at the tender age of 30. They convinced me that the best way to ensure I didn't lose everything I was just beginning to build, I should reach out and I did.

The experience was so humiliating. I was asked to verify my presence at 2 World Trade Center with means other than the standard business card and paychecks others were able to give. My salary was questioned, and it appeared that those who were there to assist me could not imagine a young, black woman earning what I was earning, although even that was still a very minimal amount for someone with my credentials and years of expertise. To make matters worse, because I was in a commission-based business, my income dropped immediately because I was injured. They refused to assist me beyond three months, and I was on my own. I know firsthand others who had received assistance with little or no questions for much longer. I had proof of expenses and evidence that I went to the hospital immediately due to my inability to breathe.

In the spirit of full transparency and after years of maturing, I must believe that in my refusal to be continually humiliated, I gave up and stop seeking the help I so desperately needed. It caused me to struggle much longer that I would have ever anticipated. It contributed to the strain on my marriage, which eventually dissolved, and it left me in a state where I stop looking for help but tried to manage life on my own. When I didn't recover in the first decade, I learned that while I was technically still working in my service industry, I would have qualified for worker's compensation. But my experience with social assistance programs was a direct contributor to something deeply entrenched within, something I still struggle with today. If someone needs help, I will do whatever I can even if it's to my detriment. I am just learning boundaries, but it served to be useful for the work we would go on to do.

Helping people preserve their dignity at moments when they needed help became the foundational edict of Generation X Community Association. Our focus became on serving the "least of them" and ensuring that they would feel the love and genuine concern from us to them. If we could ease stress in one small area, even for a moment, that was our task. It showed up in our second toy giveaway. At first, we were hesitant to press forward. However, we made up our minds and literally two weeks before Thanksgiving, we began to solicit funds to help people who were struggling and couldn't juggle providing gifts for their families during the holiday seasons. In weeks, we raised thousands of dollars, and we were able to support families by eliminating the anxiety and stress working parents carried trying to figure out how to buy something for their children when every penny they earned needed to pay the bills. The holidays can represent an expense struggling parents cannot afford. It was something near and dear to Sonji and me, growing up in a household where Santa rarely made an appearance.

The entire time, I was struggling spiritually, emotionally, economically and physically. I was grateful to be alive, and I was a woman of faith. Originally,

I felt blessed God saved me because it was His literally voice that guided me out of the building. At the same time, as the days, weeks, months and even years went by, I began to feel abandoned by God. Where are YOU? I have been faithful; I am serving You and I am doing the best I can! What do you want from me?!?!? I was both exasperated and desperate. Then He began to unfold my assignment that would drive me for the rest of my life and much of the charge given to me by God, has been lived out through the existence of Generation X Community Association. I share this with you because both the charge and this book reflect the power of community.

In addition to being called by God to preach the gospel, I was given an assignment to fight for economic justice. It was multi-layered in the objective, and it took me years to truly understand God's requirement of me. To start, I was hasty in stepping out by faith to use my financial planning expertise, life experience and the tragedy of September 11th to help minorities understand that it was not God's plan for us to sit in lack or even accept being disadvantaged based on the color of our skin. I realized I was called to help anyone who experienced trauma or catastrophic events or grew up with limited opportunities. The ask was magnanimous, and I didn't have any direction.

My life calling is clear. I am anointed to help people recover spiritually, emotionally and economically. I have been given three areas of concentration. It is the school system, the church and the prisons. I wasn't certain how to approach any of those entities, and so in the beginning, we didn't have much structure. I also didn't see an intersection for the mission fields. The one thing that was critical to the success was the access we had to the media, so we heavily leveraged our ability to produce television, which opened the doors to radio.

Progress was made immediately in both the school system and the prison. And it was through the prison system; I was able to build something that may reflect legacy. While Sherri and Jeseman are no longer active participants, it was their voice, their ideas, service and unwavering support that catapulted us into the space we find ourselves in today. But to understand it, one must truly gain some insight on the lives of Nikki and

Sonji. We used to laugh and say were like the Army, that we did more before 5am than most people did all day. We grew up where you always had to have an answer and saying we didn't know how to do something was not a viable option. So, figuring things out was what we did. In hindsight, we never approach things with moderation in mind. I am truly grateful that during my trying to find my purpose, to regain something within, Sonji never objected to any idea I brought to the table.

I was trying to honor what I believe God was telling me to do and that was to educate and empower minorities in financial literacy. I had experienced firsthand what happens when people do not anticipate the devastating impact a catastrophic event can have on a family financially. I also saw how the wealthy had plans in place that helped them to recover or at least not have finances be a detriment. It remains what is culturally deficient in our community. I began to create curriculums that would allow me to teach teenagers in high school. On behalf of the organization, I would visit Abbot District schools, which is a fancy word, for financially depressed schools or in urban disadvantaged areas. Once a month, I would educate the students on the basics of stocks, bonds, mutual funds, insurance, how to establish a bank account, what was FICA and OASDI, and the principles of financial planning.

At the same time, I wrote a book sharing my experience having survived September 11th, 2001. I was given the opportunity to share my story on major media outlets and that is how Jane Pursell, a teacher inside of Edna Mahan Correctional Facility found me. She heard my story on a major news channel, learned that I was hosting a radio show on WRSU 88.7 FM at Rutgers University and one Wednesday afternoon she called and invited me to speak to the women at the prison. What? You want me to go inside the prison? I was stuck there. Ironically, the gentleman who I worked with to gain access into the school system, Dr. DeLacy Davis, is the one I called. He was a sergeant at the East Orange Police Department and together we were making strides in the quest to impact the school system. I felt he would give me the best advice and ease any anxiety or concerns I may have had. I was correct.

When I walked through the doors of the prison, I questioned if I had anything valuable to say. Could I relay a message of resilience, perseverance and hope? What did I have to offer these women? So, I shared my story, and it worked. I survived sexual assault and child abuse. I survived giving birth to a still born and medical negligence. I survived the tragedy of September 11th and I survived financial trauma. Something in my life story had to spark hope for these women so I poured out what made me wake up daily and try to impact the world and it worked. It was after I spent time in both maximum and minimum securities, I had a private lunch in minimum securities, also known as grounds, with a group of women who poured out their institutional grievances. Then they asked me for my help.

When I returned home and eventually told the team about my day and the petition of the women, the consensus to do something was unanimous, but no one else was willing to enter the facilities. So, Generation X Community Association raised resources first and then contributed books to the library. My relationship with the prison expanded after someone asked me to participate in a program titled Focus on the Victim. This journey led me to speak at both male and female facilities throughout the entire state and over the years, I was honored to share my story as a crime victim, but also a story of resilience and how to recover from something catastrophic in one's life. I was able to both admonish and encourage thousands of incarcerated men and women that the worst decisions of their lives to that point did not have to define them. I was then given the opportunity to become a religious volunteer teaching bible study and preaching twice a month.

Generation X Community Association began to expand with volunteers willing to go inside the facilities and Bo Robinson Assessment Facilities. We honored that work until the start of Covid-19, when the world came to a screeching halt. It wasn't the work standing alone that had a major impact, it was the reality that economic justice for minorities wasn't solely about our inability to play the game of life on a level playing field. Engaging with those who were incarcerated allowed me to get to know the people. I heard about the disparate application of the law and how it impacted real people. I understood the feeling of helplessness when people talked about standing before the system guilty before getting a fair chance to defend themselves. I learned about the choices and decisions people made that caused a loss of freedom. No judgement, just someone who wanted to let them know they could live beyond their present conditions.

I thought the task was simple. In my naivety, I truly believed that if I could help formerly incarcerated people find purpose and create a lifestyle that included financial freedom, I could help anyone. After all, I was the expert. I had no idea of how challenging the assignment would really be. At the same time, after almost two decades of connecting with people who were in prison, after Covid-19, a dream to establish a learning institute was realized. The Dare 2 Dream Institute was created so that we could take a stand for the community. The goal was to serve "the least of them" and deal with real life issues that can hinder personal growth and ability to gain economic independence post-incarceration. The work was to benefit families in urban communities where formerly incarcerated individuals were seeking a second chance in life.

The Dare to Dream Institute is an entrepreneurial internship specifically designed for returning citizens who have identified a gift/skill set that can be used to create a consistent revenue stream. Instead of settling for underemployment opportunities, the returning citizen was given a change to explore the steps on how to establish a business. The internship focused on the viability of their business idea, how to create a business plan, how to build a strong support team, strategies for marketing themselves in a way that liberated them from their season of incarceration and how to reintegrate back into society. Through it all, the power of community and collaboration were pillars that we aimed to stress as major priorities.

This is their story.

FROM ADVERSITY TO ADVOCACY

A Journey of Faith, Resilience, and Purpose

Ayesha Rogers

Introduction

Every journey has its defining moments—those moments when faith, perseverance, and the will to overcome shape a life. My story is one of transformation, marked by challenges and triumphs, and guided by an unwavering belief in God's purpose for me. The path I have walked has not been easy, but each step has taught me invaluable lessons about resilience, forgiveness, and the power of community.

Reentry and Early Challenges

On June 27, 2010, I was released from Edna Mahan Correctional Facility State Prison, stepping into a world that felt both familiar and foreign. The initial joy of freedom was quickly tempered by the realities of reentry. Support from friends and family was invaluable, but stability proved elusive. When my first housing arrangement fell through, my Aunt Mae welcomed me, providing a safe haven and a reminder of the power of unconditional support. Her home became a sanctuary where I could regroup, reflect, and begin to plan my next steps.

Determined to build a new life, I sought employment and independence. My early jobs were stepping-stones, but workplace discrimination and the challenges of managing ADHD complicated my path. Despite setbacks—including the loss of benefits and the stigma of special education—I persisted. I distributed my resume, seized opportunities, and eventually secured a position that led to my first apartment. Encouraged by management, I took and passed the manager's test with a perfect score on my first attempt, demonstrating my capacity for growth and leadership.

Navigating Setbacks and Building Resilience

Success was not without adversity. Workplace dynamics forced me to leave a promising role, and the loss of my apartment, compounded by a housing scam and the passing of Aunt Mae, tested my resilience. Betrayal by family members and the struggle to maintain stability were profound challenges. Yet, through prayer and reflection, I found the strength to forgive and move forward, determined to rebuild my life with integrity.

During these turbulent times, I learned the importance of adaptability. Each setback became an opportunity to reassess my goals and strategies. I returned to familiar environments when necessary, but always kept my sights set on lasting change. The loss of my apartment was a particularly difficult blow, but it taught me to be resourceful and to seek out new opportunities even in the face of disappointment.

Achievements and Turning Points

In recent years, I have achieved milestones that reflect both personal and professional growth:

- **Passed the manager's test with a perfect score** on the first attempt, highlighting my leadership potential.
- **Earned my GED**, opening doors to further education and career advancement.
- **Graduated from the Camden College Community Health Worker program** and received my certificate for community health work—a commitment to serving others and making a positive impact in my community.
- **Received certifications and awards** for professional excellence, including recognition for my work ethic and commitment to service.
- **Honored with the University Hospital Patient Outreach Award in 2025** for outstanding community service.

- **Active member of Micah7 Ministries**, contributing to outreach and support programs.

Building on these achievements, August 2023 marked a significant new chapter when I began working with the Newark Community Street Team Organization as part of the Safe Passage initiative. In this role, I was stationed at an elementary school, where I met students where they were, prioritized their needs, and focused on their well-being. My responsibilities included case management, mentoring, and fostering positive relationships with both students and parents. Whether it was helping students improve their grades, de-escalating situations like bullying, or simply being a listening ear, I found fulfillment in being a supportive presence in the community.

Six or seven months later, I was promoted to the Victim Service Department—a role I hadn't anticipated but embraced with gratitude. Here, I worked alongside dedicated colleagues, supporting the most vulnerable members of our community: men, women, and children affected by crime and trauma. I earned certifications in victim services and even traveled to Washington, D.C., to stand in solidarity with victims and advocates. This experience was a major success in my life, deepening my understanding of community and healing.

After another six to seven months, I received a further promotion to become embedded in the University Hospital Violence Intervention Program. In this capacity, I met patients at their most vulnerable—those who had been assaulted, robbed, sexually assaulted, shot, stabbed, or otherwise victimized. My role was to provide resources and support, helping patients avoid retaliation or further victimization. Over the course of a year, I was honored with the Exceeding FY25 Award for enrolling and supporting more than 100 survivors in the HVIP Program. Every patient under my care successfully completed their individualized care plan and graduated from the program, a testament to my commitment to serving victims of crime with compassion, kindness, and respect.

These experiences at Newark Community Street Team have profoundly impacted my life, reinforcing my belief that community matters and that everyone deserves a chance to overcome obstacles and thrive—both personally and professionally.

Lessons Learned

Throughout my journey, several key lessons have emerged:

- **Resilience is built through adversity.** Each setback became an opportunity to grow stronger and more determined. I learned that challenges are not roadblocks but stepping-stones to greater achievements.
- **Faith provides direction and hope.** Trusting in God's plan gave me the courage to persevere when circumstances seemed insurmountable. My faith has been a source of comfort and inspiration, guiding me through difficult times and helping me to maintain a positive outlook.
- **Forgiveness is essential for healing.** Letting go of resentment allowed me to move forward and embrace new possibilities. I discovered that forgiveness is not just about others, but about freeing myself from the burden of anger and regret.
- **Support networks matter.** The unwavering support of individuals like Aunt Mae and my pastor at Micah7 Ministries was instrumental in my recovery and growth. Their encouragement and guidance helped me to stay focused on my goals and to believe in my own potential.
- **Self-advocacy is powerful.** Pursuing education, certifications, and leadership roles empowered me to redefine my future. I learned to speak up for myself, to seek out resources, and to take initiative in shaping my own destiny.

The Role of Community

One of the most profound lessons I have learned is the transformative power of a strong community. Throughout my journey, I have been blessed to be part of communities that offered support, encouragement, and a sense of belonging. Whether it was the warmth of Aunt Mae's home, the camaraderie of my colleagues at ShopRite, or the spiritual fellowship at Micah7 Ministries, these communities provided the foundation upon which I could rebuild my life.

Community is more than just a group of people—it is a network of relationships, shared values, and mutual support. In times of crisis, the community offers comfort and practical assistance. In moments of triumph, it celebrates achievements and encourages further growth. My experiences have shown me that no one succeeds alone; we all rely on the strength and generosity of others to help us reach our goals.

Being part of a strong community has also inspired me to give back. I have made it a priority to support others who are facing challenges, to offer mentorship and guidance, and to contribute to the well-being of those around me. Through volunteer work, outreach programs, and everyday acts of kindness, I strive to create a positive and inclusive environment where everyone has the opportunity to thrive.

Vision for the Future

Looking ahead, I am excited to begin college classes at Essex County College in 2026, where I will pursue a degree in social work. My goal is to leverage my experiences and education to advocate for individuals who feel unseen or marginalized. I am committed to using my story and testimony to inspire others, demonstrating that adversity can be transformed into strength and purpose.

My vision is to work within my community, providing support, resources, and guidance to those facing similar challenges. I aspire to become a licensed social worker, specializing in outreach and rehabilitation, and to collaborate with organizations dedicated to social justice and mental health. In addition to my academic pursuits, I plan to continue my involvement with Micah7 Ministries and other faith-based organizations, offering mentorship and support to individuals navigating reentry and recovery. My long-term objective is to establish a nonprofit organization focused on empowerment, education, and holistic healing.

I am also passionate about developing programs that address the unique needs of formerly incarcerated individuals, those living with ADHD, and others who have experienced trauma or systemic barriers. By sharing my experiences and insights, I hope to create resources and opportunities that empower others to overcome obstacles and achieve their full potential.

Expanding Horizons

As I prepare to embark on this new chapter, I am mindful of the importance of continuous learning and personal growth. College will provide me with the knowledge and skills necessary to make a meaningful impact in the field of social work. I am eager to engage with professors, classmates, and community leaders to exchange ideas and collaborate on initiatives that promote social justice and equity.

My commitment to service extends beyond my professional aspirations. I believe that true leadership is rooted in humility, empathy, and a willingness to listen. By remaining open to new perspectives and experiences, I hope to become a more effective advocate and ally for those in need.

Conclusion: The Power of a Strong Community

My journey is ongoing, and I look forward to embracing new opportunities, building stronger communities, and living out my purpose with compassion and integrity. Every challenge I have faced has prepared me for the work ahead, and I am dedicated to helping others realize their potential and achieve lasting change. Through faith, perseverance, and a commitment to service, I am confident that I can make a meaningful impact—one life, one story, one chapter at a time.

Above all, I have learned that the power of a strong community is transformative. It is through the support, encouragement, and shared purpose of those around us that we find the strength to overcome adversity and create lasting change. Community is the bedrock upon which dreams are built and sustained. It is the source of hope in times of despair, the catalyst for growth in moments of uncertainty, and the foundation for a future filled with possibility.

As I continue my journey, I am committed to nurturing and strengthening the communities to which I belong. I will strive to be a source of support and inspiration for others, fostering connections that uplift and empower, and contributing to a legacy of compassion and resilience. Together, we can build a world where everyone has the opportunity to thrive and where the bonds of community illuminate the path to a brighter tomorrow.

LEAVING CRUMBS IN THE WILDERNESS FOR OTHERS TO FOLLOW

Damon Venable

Introduction: The Weight of Freedom

On May 4, 2021, I stepped out of East Jersey State Prison—Rahway State Prison—after thirty-five years behind bars. I was sixteen when I entered, and now, at fifty-one, the world outside was a kaleidoscope of color and sound, overwhelming in its intensity. The air tasted different, the sky seemed impossibly wide, and every step felt like both a victory and a risk. Freedom, I quickly learned, was not a finish line—it was a new beginning, fraught with uncertainty and possibility.

I remember the first breath I took as a free man. It was sharp, cold, and filled with the scent of spring. My family stood waiting, their faces a blend of joy and worry. I wanted to run to them, to collapse into their arms, but something held me back—a fear that I was no longer the person they remembered. Thirty-five years is a lifetime. I had missed birthdays, graduations, funerals, and the slow, everyday moments that knit a family together.

Yet, even as I tasted the sweetness of release, the bitter reality of systemic oppression quickly reasserted itself. Lifetime parole meant perpetual surveillance, restrictions, and the constant threat of having my freedom revoked. My joy was extinguished almost immediately, replaced by a sense of being shackled in a different way. The attitudes of parole officers—belligerent, disrespectful, and antagonistic—reminded me that the carceral state's grip extended far beyond prison walls. I was free, but not truly free.

Achievements: Building Success Against the Odds

Despite these challenges, I refused to let my spirit be crushed. My journey toward redemption and transformation had begun long before my release. Inside prison, I cultivated a mindset of success, believing that my vision of myself could manifest in reality. I survived the brutality of the adult prison system as a child, emerging as a healthy, educated Black man with a supportive family waiting for me.

The first days outside were a blur. I was overwhelmed by the rush of traffic, the constant hum of technology, and the sheer pace of life. I felt like a relic from another era, unsure how to navigate a world that had moved on without me. My confidence wavered, and for the first time in decades, I was genuinely scared—not of physical harm, but of failing in the free world. Yet, I knew I had to overcome this funk. I reached out to friends who had been released before me, reconnected with family, and began building a network of support.

One of the most significant achievements was my ability to turn adversity into opportunity. When my parole officer mandated participation in a reentry program run by a private, for-profit organization, I initially resisted. The program was not authorized by the board that released me, and I felt coerced. Nevertheless, I chose to make the best of the situation, using it as a chance to network and learn.

Through this program, I met professionals who would profoundly impact my trajectory. I took advantage of every opportunity for business and financial literacy, professional development, and job readiness training. My determination to succeed set me apart, and I became known for my drive and commitment. I collected business cards, signed up for training, and immersed myself in the world of reentry services.

This proactive approach paid off. I was able to fortuitously reconnect with someone whose story had made an indelible and powerful impression on me while I was in prison. The Reverend Dr. Nicole B. Simpson, CEO of the

Dare 2 Dream Institute, while performing her prison ministry initiative, entered into a NJDOC prison I was in and shared her personal story of childhood traumas and overcoming a variety of calamity and adversity in her life. The power, the humility, and the compassion she evinced that day while recounting the most deeply traumatic experiences in her life impacted me so profoundly that it accelerated my growth and maturity as a man. And she continues to positively impact me through her organization that honed my entrepreneurial skills and financial literacy, eventually helping me become the owner and operator of my second LLC as an author, reentry consultant, and motivational speaker. Additionally, my contacts with the Urban League of the Greater Union County provided mentorship, peer navigation, and assistance in overcoming legal barriers and securing essential documents for citizenship and identification.

Lessons Learned: The Power of Mindset and Community

The journey was not without setbacks. My criminal background made it difficult to secure employment in professional fields. Employers were reluctant to take a chance on me, fearing the risk. Instead of succumbing to frustration, I doubled down on my resolve. I increased my volunteerism and networking, demonstrating reliability, dependability, and adaptability. Through these efforts, I secured references for job openings, educational opportunities, and business contracts.

The most important lesson I learned was the necessity of self-care and realistic expectations. Managing post-release life required a clear understanding of my goals, a tangible plan for achievement, and a commitment to maintaining my mental, physical, and spiritual health. Inside prison, I was disciplined about exercise and nutrition; outside, I struggled to maintain that discipline. Seeking an accountability partner helped me stay on track, reinforcing the idea that no one succeeds alone.

Another crucial lesson was the importance of reconnecting with family and friends. Healing from the trauma of long-term incarceration required therapy, counseling, and honest conversations about expectations and accountability. Building strong social and professional relationships was essential for happiness and progress.

I learned to forgive myself for the years lost and to celebrate the victories, no matter how small. Each day outside was a gift, but also a challenge. I had to relearn how to trust, how to hope, and how to dream.

The Role of the Returning Citizens Community

One of the greatest opportunities for post-release success was relying on the support of the Returning Citizens community. This network of likeminded individuals—entrepreneurs, counselors, mentors, social service providers, community organizers, legal advocates, business owners, parents, teachers, property owners, taxpayers, board members, pastors, and community leaders—operates on principles of self-reliance, cooperation, and mutual support.

Upon returning home, I was struck by the economic disarray in my community. Most store owners and merchants did not look like me, speak my language, or share my culture. This lack of investment in the Black community's economic strength was a painful reality. It was through the Returning Citizens community that I found purpose and mission, engaging in real conversations about the challenges we faced and the need to uplift others through example.

I learned that no one should have to travel the post-incarceration journey alone. While each person's experience is unique, having companions, mentors, and guides is not just beneficial—it is essential. The community provided a reservoir of competent, invested individuals who supported my success as much as I supported theirs.

I remember sitting in a church basement, surrounded by men and women who had walked the same path. We shared stories, laughed at our mistakes, and offered advice. There was a sense of belonging, a feeling that we were building something together—a future where our pasts did not define us.

Specific Achievements: Professional and Personal Growth

My achievements since release are a testament to the power of mindset and community. I earned three college degrees while incarcerated, demonstrating my commitment to education and personal growth. I became an author, sharing my story to inspire others. As a reentry consultant and motivational speaker, I used my experiences to help others navigate the challenges of post-release life.

I secured employment with a state legal agency, continuing my lifelong commitment to service by assisting others with legal issues. Volunteering with various organizations allowed me to showcase my skills and reliability, leading to professional opportunities and contracts for my business. I built a network of mentors, peers, and supporters who provided guidance, encouragement, and practical assistance.

Through the Dare 2 Dream Institute and the Urban League of the Greater Union County, I developed entrepreneurial skills, financial literacy, and professional confidence. These organizations helped me overcome legal barriers, obtain essential documents, and pursue my goals with determination and resilience.

One of my proudest moments was standing before a group of young men, sharing my story and watching their faces light up with hope. I saw myself in them—the uncertainty, the fear, the longing for a second chance. I told them, "Your past does not have to be your future. You can build something new, something beautiful."

Practical Strategies for Success

Success after incarceration is not a matter of luck—it is the result of deliberate choices, persistent effort, and strategic planning. Here are practical strategies that helped me and can help others on a similar journey:

1. Develop a Clear Vision and Set Realistic Goals

The first step is to define what success means to you. For me, it was not just about financial stability, but about personal growth, service, and community impact. Set short-term and long-term goals, and break them down into actionable steps. Write them down, revisit them regularly, and adjust as needed.

I kept a notebook where I wrote my dreams, my fears, and my plans. Each goal was a stepping-stone, a way to measure progress and stay motivated.

2. Build a Support Network

No one succeeds alone. Reach out to family, friends, mentors, and organizations such as the Dare 2 Dream Institute and the Urban League of Greater Union County. Attend community meetings, workshops, and networking events. Surround yourself with people who believe in your potential and are willing to offer guidance, encouragement, and accountability.

I found my greatest allies in unexpected places—a neighbor who offered a job, a pastor who listened without judgment, a fellow returning citizen who became my business partner.

3. Embrace Lifelong Learning

Education is a powerful tool for transformation. Take advantage of every opportunity to learn—whether it's formal education, vocational training, or self-study. Read books, attend seminars, and seek out online courses. Stay curious and open to new ideas.

I enrolled in online classes, attended workshops, and read everything I could get my hands on. Knowledge became my armor against doubt and fear.

4. Practice Self-Care and Wellness

Physical, mental, and spiritual health are the foundation of success. Develop routines for exercise, nutrition, meditation, and rest. Seek therapy or counseling if needed. Find an accountability partner to help you stay on track. Remember, self-care is not selfish—it's essential.

I started each day with a walk, a prayer, and a moment of reflection. I learned to listen to my body and my heart, to rest when I was weary, and to seek help when I was struggling.

5. Volunteer and Give Back

Volunteering is a way to build skills, expand your network, and contribute to your community. It demonstrates reliability and commitment and often leads to professional opportunities. Look for organizations that align with your values and interests.

I volunteered at food banks, mentored young people, and helped organize community events. Each act of service was a way to heal, to connect, and to grow.

6. Network Relentlessly

Collect business cards, connect on social media, and follow up with people you meet. Attend job fairs, workshops, and community events. Networking opens doors to jobs, contracts, and collaborations. Be proactive and persistent.

I learned that every conversation was an opportunity. I followed up, stayed in touch, and built relationships that lasted.

7. Turn Adversity into Opportunity

Every challenge is a chance to grow. When faced with obstacles—like mandated programs or employment barriers—look for ways to learn, connect, and advance your goals. Adaptability and resilience are key.

I turned setbacks into lessons, failures into fuel. Each obstacle was a test of my resolve, a chance to prove that I could rise above my circumstances.

8. Seek Out Mentorship

Mentors provide wisdom, perspective, and support. Find people who have walked a similar path and are willing to share their experiences. Be open to feedback and willing to learn from others' successes and mistakes.

My mentors were my guides, my sounding boards, my champions. They challenged me, encouraged me, and celebrated my victories.

9. Document Your Journey

Keep a journal of your experiences, achievements, and lessons learned. This not only helps you reflect and grow, but can inspire others. Sharing your story—through writing, speaking, or mentoring—creates a ripple effect of hope and possibility.

I wrote every day, capturing the highs and lows, the triumphs and the tears. My story became my legacy, a breadcrumb trail for others to follow.

10. Advocate for Yourself and Others

Learn about your rights and resources. Speak up when you encounter injustice or barriers. Advocate for policy changes that benefit returning citizens. Use your voice to uplift others and create systemic change.

I joined advocacy groups, spoke at public forums, and worked to change policies that kept people trapped in cycles of poverty and incarceration.

Overcoming Challenges: Strategies in Action

The challenges of post-release life are numerous, but they are manageable with the right approach. Believing in oneself, setting realistic expectations, and developing a game plan are essential. Self-care—mental, physical, and spiritual—is paramount. Seeking accountability partners, mentors, and community support helps maintain motivation and discipline.

Networking and volunteerism are powerful tools for overcoming barriers. Demonstrating reliability, adaptability, and commitment opens doors to professional opportunities. Building strong relationships with family, friends, and community members provides emotional support and practical assistance.

Healing from the trauma of incarceration requires therapy, counseling, and honest conversations. Reconnecting with loved ones and building new relationships fosters happiness and progress. Surrounding oneself with successful, supportive people creates an environment conducive to growth and achievement.

I faced setbacks—jobs lost, opportunities denied, moments of doubt. But each time, I returned to my strategies, my community, and my faith. I learned that resilience is not just about surviving, but about thriving.

Conclusion: The Power of a Strong Community

I am still far from my personal measure of success, but I know I am on the right path. My community, friends, and colleagues continually acknowledge and appreciate my efforts to help others. Whatever your aspirations and ambitions, make sure one of them is to be an example for others—to be the living breadcrumb in the wilderness for others to follow.

Success is not determined by money, status, or material possessions. The most valuable asset is time—use it wisely and for good causes. The journey from incarceration to freedom is arduous, but with the right mindset, support, and community, it is possible to achieve greatness.

The Returning Citizens community exemplifies the power of collective strength, resilience, and mutual support. By relying on each other, sharing experiences, and uplifting one another, we create a foundation for success that extends beyond individual achievement. Together, we leave crumbs in the wilderness for others to follow, lighting the path to freedom, purpose, and fulfillment.

RISING FROM THE ASHES

A Journey of Resilience and Community

Fawn Stratton

Introduction: The Power of Perseverance

Life, as I have come to know it, is a series of battles—some fought in silence, others in the open. My story is not just about survival, but about transformation, hope, and the relentless pursuit of a better tomorrow. I share this chapter not only to recount my journey but to inspire those who feel lost, broken, or alone. Through every hardship, I discovered that the strength to rise comes not only from within but also from the embrace of a caring community.

Early Years: Abandonment and the Search for Love

From the very beginning, my life was marked by abandonment. As a baby, my mother left me, and I was placed in the loving arms of Mrs. R. Bowmen, a foster mother who became my sanctuary. Her home was filled with warmth, safety, and unconditional love. I remember Sunday mornings—dressing up for church, the smell of home-cooked meals, and the gentle touch of someone who truly cared. These moments were fleeting, but they planted seeds of hope that would carry me through the darkest times.

At age ten, everything changed. I was taken from Mrs. Bowmen and thrust back into the chaos of my biological family—a place where love was replaced by violence and neglect. The abuse was relentless: extension cords, belts, fists, and even a hot iron left marks not only on my body but on my soul. School became a refuge, yet even there, I was forced to hide the truth, inventing stories to explain bruises and scars. The pain of betrayal by those meant to protect me was profound, but it taught me early

Lessons in Survival: Foster Homes and Finding Faith

My journey through the foster care system was turbulent. Some homes offered kindness and stability, while others exposed me to new dangers. In Cliffwood, I found a family who embraced me, teaching me about faith and resilience. Their love was a balm, but anger and trauma sometimes erupted, leading to more moves and more heartbreak. Each transition forced me to adapt, to learn, and to fight for my sense of self.

Faith became my anchor. Even as a child, I played "church," laying hands and praying for others, not knowing that these rituals would one day become my lifeline. In moments of despair, I turned to God, seeking answers and comfort. The lessons learned in those foster homes—about forgiveness, hope, and the possibility of change—became the foundation for my future.

Adolescence: Trials, Mistakes, and the Road to Redemption

By fourteen, I was experimenting with drugs, seeking escape from pain. Selling and using became a way to survive, to numb the hurt. At seventeen, a miscarriage and a rape shattered my world further. Shame and fear kept me silent, but I pressed on, determined to carve out a life for myself. I found work, supported myself, and tried to build a future, even as the shadows of my past loomed large.

Motherhood brought new challenges. My daughter was born from circumstances I wished I could change, and I struggled to be the mother she deserved. The cycle of addiction and incarceration threatened to consume me, but each setback became a lesson. I learned that mistakes do not define us—they are opportunities to grow, to change, and to seek redemption.

Achievements: Breaking the Cycle and Building a New Life

Emerging from the shadows of addiction and incarceration, my first achievement was simply choosing a different path. After my release from prison, I stood at a crossroads—one direction led back to old habits, the other toward an uncertain future. I chose uncertainty, determined never to return to the life that had nearly destroyed me. That decision, though quiet and unseen, was the first act of defiance against a system that expected my failure.

Finding Work and Building Skills

My initial jobs were humble but transformative. Roofing in the sweltering summer heat taught me discipline and endurance. Each morning, I rose before dawn, my hands raw and aching, but my spirit growing stronger. Cooking in a local diner brought new lessons—teamwork, patience, and the satisfaction of serving others. I learned to take pride in small victories: a roof completed, a meal well-cooked, a paycheck earned honestly. These experiences laid the groundwork for my future, instilling a sense of self-worth that had long been missing.

Entrepreneurship: Creating My Own Business

The leap into entrepreneurship was both terrifying and exhilarating. With little more than determination and a handful of savings, I started my own cleaning business. The early days were a whirlwind of challenges—securing clients, managing finances, and learning the intricacies of running a company. I faced skepticism from others and moments of self-doubt, but each contract signed was a victory. Over time, my business grew, providing not only for my family but also for others in my community who needed work. Becoming a business owner was more than a professional milestone; it was a declaration that my past would not dictate my future.

Academic Success: Pursuing Higher Education

Encouraged by friends and mentors, I enrolled in college to pursue a degree in Human Social Services. The transition was daunting—balancing coursework with work and family responsibilities, battling health setbacks like abscesses and cancer, and overcoming the lingering effects of trauma. Yet, I persevered. I spent countless nights studying, fueled by the desire to help others who had walked similar paths. Making the Dean's List was a moment of profound pride; it was proof that I could excel in a world that once seemed closed to me. Receiving awards for academic achievement and completing an internship where I supported others in crisis were not just personal victories—they were testaments to the power of resilience and the importance of giving back.

Mentorship and Community Leadership

As my confidence grew, so did my commitment to uplifting others. I became a mentor to those struggling with addiction, incarceration, and trauma. Through Dare 2 Dream Institute, I completed a program focused on personal development and community engagement. I led workshops, shared my story, and offered guidance to those who felt hopeless. Seeing others find their footing and begin their own journeys of transformation became one of my greatest achievements. The ripple effect of hope and empowerment extended far beyond my own life.

Rebuilding Family Bonds

Perhaps the most meaningful achievement was rebuilding my relationship with my daughter and grandsons. Years of pain and misunderstanding had created a gulf between us, but through honest conversations and shared experiences, we began to heal. Moving to Atlanta to be closer to them marked a new chapter. Our bond, once fragile, grew stronger with each passing day. Family dinners, laughter, and the simple joy of being present for one another became the foundation of our renewed connection.

Giving Back: Service and Advocacy

With stability came a sense of responsibility. I volunteered at local shelters, participated in community outreach programs, and advocated for policy changes to support those in foster care and recovery. My business provided jobs for people facing barriers to employment, and I worked with organizations to create pathways for others to succeed. Each act of service reinforced the belief that true achievement is measured not only by personal success but by the impact we have on others.

Lessons Learned: The Importance of Self-Worth, Forgiveness, and Growth

Claiming Self-Worth Through Struggle

One of the most profound lessons I learned is that self-worth is not something others can bestow—it must be claimed through struggle, reflection, and perseverance. For years, I measured my value by the opinions of those around me, especially those who failed to protect or nurture me. The journey through foster homes, addiction, and incarceration left me feeling broken and unworthy. It was only through facing my pain head-on—acknowledging the scars, both visible and invisible—that I began to understand my own strength.

I remember sitting alone in a small apartment after my release from prison, surrounded by reminders of past mistakes. The silence was heavy, but in that quiet, I found the courage to ask myself: "What do I want my life to mean?" The answer was not immediate, but it came through small acts—showing up for work, caring for my daughter, and refusing to let setbacks define me. Each time I chose hope over despair, I reclaimed a piece of my self-worth.

The Power and Necessity of Forgiveness

Forgiveness was another essential lesson, and perhaps the hardest to learn. The wounds inflicted by family, strangers, and even myself ran deep. For years, I carried anger and resentment, believing that holding onto pain would somehow protect me. But I discovered that forgiveness is not about excusing harm—it's about freeing yourself from its grip.

Forgiving those who hurt me required confronting the past without flinching. I wrote letters I never sent, spoke words aloud in empty rooms, and prayed for the strength to let go. The process was messy and nonlinear, but each step brought relief. Most importantly, I learned to forgive myself—for the choices I made in survival mode, for the times I failed those I loved, and for the years lost to addiction and fear. Self-forgiveness opened the door to healing and allowed me to move forward with compassion.

Resilience: Adapting and Overcoming

Resilience became my lifeline. Life's challenges did not end with sobriety or success; new obstacles emerged at every turn. Health crises, financial setbacks, and the ongoing work of rebuilding relationships tested my resolve. But each trial reinforced the lesson that resilience is not about never falling—it's about rising every time you do.

I learned to adapt, to seek help when needed, and to celebrate progress, no matter how small. The support of mentors, friends, and community members was invaluable. Their encouragement reminded me that resilience is often a collective effort, strengthened by the bonds we form with others.

The Transformative Power of Community

Community played a vital role in my journey. From foster families to church members, sponsors, and friends, each person who offered support became a thread in the tapestry of my recovery. Their belief in me, even when I doubted myself, was a lifeline. I learned that asking for help is not a sign of weakness but of courage. Together, we can overcome obstacles that seem insurmountable on our own.

Joining Dare 2 Dream Institute and participating in community outreach programs taught me the value of collective healing. I witnessed firsthand how shared stories and mutual support could transform lives. Community is not just a safety net—it's a source of inspiration, accountability, and hope. Through service and advocacy, I found purpose beyond my own recovery, helping others discover their strength and resilience.

Growth Through Education and Service

Education was another pillar of growth. Returning to school as an adult was daunting, but it taught me discipline, curiosity, and the joy of learning. Making the Dean's List and earning awards were affirmations of my ability, but the true reward was the opportunity to help others through my internship and volunteer work. Service became a way to give back, to honor those who had supported me, and to create pathways for others to succeed.

Through mentoring, advocacy, and community leadership, I learned that growth is a lifelong process. Each new challenge is an opportunity to learn, adapt, and become a better version of yourself.

Practical Wisdom for Others

Ask for help: Seeking support is a sign of strength, not weakness.
No one succeeds alone. Throughout my journey, the moments that changed my life most profoundly were those when I reached out—whether to a foster parent, a mentor, or a member of Dare 2 Dream Institute. Asking for help opened doors to healing and opportunity. It's not easy to admit vulnerability, but it's the first step toward building genuine connections and finding the resources you need. If you're struggling, remember that there are people and organizations ready to support you. Your courage to ask can inspire others to do the same.

Forgive yourself and others: Healing begins with letting go of resentment.
Forgiveness is a process, not a single act. I learned that holding onto anger and regret only deepened my wounds. Writing unsent letters, speaking my pain aloud, and seeking spiritual guidance helped me release the grip of resentment. Forgiving those who hurt you doesn't mean excusing their actions—it means freeing yourself to move forward. Equally important is self-forgiveness: accepting your past mistakes, understanding why you made them, and choosing to grow. This act of compassion toward yourself is essential for true healing.

Celebrate small victories: Progress is often incremental; honor each step.
Recovery and growth rarely happen overnight. My achievements—earning a paycheck, completing a class, reconnecting with family—were built on countless small steps. Celebrate every milestone, no matter how minor it

seems. These moments of progress are proof of your resilience and determination. By acknowledging your growth, you build confidence and motivation to keep moving forward. Share your victories with your community; their encouragement will amplify your sense of accomplishment.

Stay connected: Community provides strength, accountability, and hope.
Isolation breeds despair, but connection fosters hope. The support I found in foster families, church groups, and especially Dare 2 Dream Institute was transformative. Community is not just a network—it's a lifeline. Stay engaged with those who uplift you, whether through support groups, volunteering, or simply sharing your story. Accountability partners and mentors can help you stay focused on your goals, while collective celebration and shared struggles remind you that you're never alone. Lean into these relationships; they are the foundation of lasting change.

Never stop learning: Education and service open doors to growth and fulfillment.
Returning to school as an adult was daunting, but it reignited my curiosity and sense of purpose. Education—formal or informal—expands your horizons and equips you to help others. Service, whether through volunteering or mentoring, deepens your understanding and strengthens your community. Every new skill, lesson, or act of kindness is a step toward a more fulfilling life. Embrace lifelong learning and seek opportunities to give back; you'll find that growth and fulfillment are intertwined.

The Power of Community: Rebuilding and Giving Back

Moving to Atlanta to be with my daughter and grandsons marked a new chapter. Our relationship, strained by the past, began to heal through honest conversations and shared experiences. Joining Dare 2 Dream Institute and completing the program was a milestone, but the true achievement was becoming part of a community dedicated to uplifting others.

As a business owner and mentor, I strive to inspire those who feel hopeless. My story is proof that no matter how many times you fall, you can rise again. The support of a strong community—people who see your potential and encourage your growth—is the greatest gift. Together, we create spaces where healing, learning, and transformation are possible.

Conclusion: The Transformative Power of Community

My journey is far from over. I continue to face challenges, but I do so with the knowledge that I am not alone. The lessons learned—about resilience, forgiveness, and the power of community—guide me every day. If there is one truth that stands above all, it is this: community is the foundation upon which hope and healing are built.

Throughout my life, it was the embrace of others—foster families, mentors, friends, and the members of Dare 2 Dream Institute—that gave me the strength to rise after every fall. Community is more than a safety net; it is a source of inspiration, accountability, and belonging. In moments of despair, it was the encouragement of those around me that helped me persevere. In times of triumph, it was their celebration that made my victories meaningful.

At Dare 2 Dream Institute, I witnessed firsthand how shared stories and mutual support could transform lives. By participating in workshops, outreach, and advocacy, I became part of a movement dedicated to uplifting others. The ripple effect of hope and empowerment extended far beyond my own life, touching families, neighborhoods, and future generations.

To anyone reading this, know that you are worthy of love, success, and happiness. Surround yourself with people who lift you up, seek help when you need it, and never give up on yourself. True strength is found in unity—in the bonds we form, the support we offer, and the communities we build together. My story is just one among many, but it is a testament to the enduring power of hope and the strength found in community. Together, we can create spaces where healing, learning, and transformation are not only possible but inevitable.

FROM NUMBER TO NAME

A Journey of Triumph and Community

Jasmine Wilkes

"Even the very hairs on your head are all numbered."— Matthew 10:30, NIV

Introduction: Becoming a Number

On November 21, 2000, at just 21 years old, I entered the New Jersey Department of Corrections. My identity was reduced to #41337—a number that would define me for the next seventeen years. The trauma of incarceration is rarely spoken about; the system focuses on the crime, not the person or the pain that led them there. My journey is one of reclaiming identity, healing, and ultimately, transformation.

The Weight of a Number

Numbers have a way of sticking with you. They can be markers of achievement, like a student ID, or reminders of pain, like a prison number. For years, #41337 was my reality. I could not remember my own social security number, but I could recall my state number with corrections instantly. That number was a constant reminder of the trauma endured—silent night cries, violence, hate, and mental and physical abuse. Yet, behind every state number lies a story, a person, and a set of circumstances that led them there. My story is not just about surviving the system, but about breaking free from it and building a life worth living.

The Halfway House: A Bridge Between Worlds

In 2015, I was released from Edna Mahan Correctional Facility for Women and transferred to the Millicent Fenwick House in Paterson—a halfway house for incarcerated women nearing parole. The halfway house was meant to be a step toward freedom, but it came with its own set of challenges. I was still miles away from home, in a city I didn't know, separated from my family in South Jersey. The program was structured as a drug rehabilitation program, requiring daily group sessions and weekly Narcotics Anonymous meetings. While I was not battling addiction, I participated fully, recognizing that every step forward was a step toward reclaiming my life.

Walking to those meetings, I absorbed my surroundings—a world that felt brand new after more than a decade behind bars. I noticed how people dressed, the cars they drove, and the rhythm of daily life. My mind wandered, searching for my place in this new chapter. I didn't know how to use a cell phone or navigate the internet. The world had changed, and I had to catch up.

Levels of Progress

The halfway house operated on a tiered system. The first level required weeks of in-house groups and meetings. With good behavior and attendance, I earned the privilege to attend school and seek employment. I enrolled at Passaic County Community College for Human Services and, thanks to a referral from Mrs. McNeil—a seasoned counselor—I landed a job as a server at Mr. G's Diner. Mr. G was more than an employer; he was a mentor, a community leader, and a source of wisdom. He treated me with kindness and respect, always asking how I was doing—not just as an employee, but as a person. Working for him helped me feel human again.

Achievements: Building a New Life

Education and Career

Balancing work and studies, I gradually shed the psychological chains of my prison number. I gained new numbers—student ID, bank account, and, most importantly, a release date. My exposure to the world outside helped erase the psychological chains associated with #41337. I was no longer defined by my past; I was building a future.

On Saturdays, I would go to the college library to access a computer and complete my schoolwork. Sundays were often spent working double shifts at the diner, eager to be out of the house and earning money. These experiences were more than just steps toward independence—they were milestones in my journey of self-discovery and empowerment.

Spiritual Support and Community

My pastor, Dr. Nicole B. Simpson, was a frequent visitor during my stay at Fenwick. Her visits provided spiritual support and a sense of belonging. She introduced me to Micah 7 Ministries, a church founded on hope and justice for the oppressed. The church's mission resonated deeply with me, and I found solace in its message of restoration and divine compassion. Community became a cornerstone in my journey, offering support, encouragement, and a sense of purpose.

Release and Reentry

My release date was set for March 6, 2017, under the No Early Release Act. However, I was granted release a day early—March 5, 2017. The significance of that extra day was not lost on me; it was an answered prayer, a testament to faith and resilience. My sisters came to pick me up, and the ride home was filled with anxiety and anticipation. After seventeen years in prison, freedom was both exhilarating and overwhelming. I experienced an anxiety attack during the ride, a stark reminder that reentry is not just a physical transition but an emotional one as well.

Reconnecting with my sisters was both joyful and challenging. They had grown up while I was away, and in many ways, we were strangers. I had to learn their routines, their personalities, and how to fit into their lives. They, in turn, had to adjust to the woman I had become—a woman shaped by years of hardship, faith, and determination.

Lessons Learned: Resilience, Identity, and Faith

The Reality of Reentry

Everyone dreams about the day of their release while in prison. My visions of release changed over the years—from celebrations with friends to limousine rides with loved ones. The reality was different. Both of my parents had passed away while I was incarcerated, and my grandmother and immediate family had moved out of state. My sister Camille and her husband stayed in New Jersey so I would have a place to come home to. Their sacrifice was a powerful reminder of the importance of family and community.

After moving in with my sisters, I used spring break to adjust to the real world. They taught me how to use a cell phone, navigate self-checkout at stores, and manage daily life. Once classes resumed, I commuted weekly from South Jersey to North Jersey, staying at a hotel for classes and relying on Uber for transportation. I lived off my savings from the halfway house, but freedom brought new financial challenges.

Reconnecting and Building Relationships

Social media allowed me to reconnect with my first love, Khayree. Our reunion was a source of joy and comfort, and he became a significant part of my life as I commuted to school. After the semester ended, my savings ran out, and I faced new challenges—finding a job, securing my own place, and building a life outside of my sister's home.

Five months after my release, I found work as a server at Applebee's Restaurant in Westampton, New Jersey. Working for tips, I prayed before and during each shift, trusting that God would provide. I established a savings account and spent only what was necessary for basic needs and transportation. In October 2017, I purchased my own car—a 2007 Jeep Laredo. By December, I moved into my own apartment in Pennsauken, New

Jersey. It was a modest one-bedroom above a storefront, but it was mine—a symbol of independence and resilience.

Becoming a Homeowner

One of the most significant achievements in my journey was becoming a homeowner. After working as a mobile phlebotomist for a year, my supervisor shared that she was moving, and her house would be available for rent. She connected me with her landlord, and the rent was more than affordable for us. We relocated from our one-bedroom apartment above a store to a three-story, five-bedroom house. The mailbox was a vintage Disney mailbox with Mickey Mouse and friends—a sign that this home was meant to be, especially since my son Khayree Jr. adored Mickey Mouse. This move was more than just a change of address; it marked a transformation from transient living to stability and from uncertainty to security. While renting a house, we learned firsthand about the challenges of homeownership. There were nights we worried about leaky pipes and mornings spent shoveling snow before work, all while budgeting carefully to make ends meet. I still remember the first time Khayree Jr. and I unpacked his boxes in his new room—he lined up his Mickey Mouse toys along the windowsill and danced with excitement, making the space feel truly ours. Our neighbors greeted us warmly, bringing welcome treats and encouraging words that helped us feel part of the community. In January 2026, we were blessed to become owners in the same community—just blocks from where we had always dreamed of living. Becoming a homeowner was a testament to perseverance, faith, and the unwavering support of those around me.

Creative Expression and Empowerment

In April 2018, my book "Fears, Years & Tears of Da'Diva" was published by Harvest Wealth Publishing. The book was a collection of poetry and reflections written during my incarceration. Writing was my therapy, a way to process pain and find hope. Publishing the book was never my intention, but it became a platform for sharing my story and empowering others.

Invitations to speak at events followed, and I embraced the opportunity to use my voice for change.

Motherhood and New Beginnings

Khayree moved in with me in the summer of 2018, and together we built a life filled with love and laughter. At 40 years old, I became pregnant with our son, Khayree Jr.—my "inevitable miracle." Motherhood was a dream come true, a blessing I had prayed for over the years. The birth of my son brought new purpose and fulfillment, and I embraced the challenges and joys of raising a child.

The pandemic brought unexpected changes. I was laid off from Applebee's and received unemployment benefits, allowing me to stay home with my baby. I used this time to pursue a certification in phlebotomy, passing the National Health Association test and becoming a certified phlebotomy technician. I found work as a mobile phlebotomist, performing COVID-19 testing at various facilities and training new hires. My supervisor helped me find a new home—a three-story, five-bedroom house with a vintage Disney mailbox, a sign that it was meant to be.

After a year as a mobile phlebotomist, I joined Virtua Memorial Hospital as a team lead in the COVID unit, testing pre-op patients and non-vaccinated employees. The position offered stability, flexibility, and a pay increase.

In January 2022, Khayree and I were married at Micah 7 Ministries. It was a small, intimate ceremony with close friends and family. Three months into our marriage, I became pregnant with our second son, Kobe Josiah Wilkes—my "Kwaanza baby." Watching my children grow and play together fills my heart with gratitude. There was a time when it was just me and God, but now I am blessed to be a wife and mother.

Professional Growth and Education

To date, I am a certified medical billing and coding specialist, working for a reputable Revenue Cycle Management Company as a billing representative. My role involves processing claims for secondary insurance. I am a recent graduate of Devry University, with an associate degree in Health Information Technology. I am currently pursuing a bachelor's degree in health information management, with certification in Registered Health Information Administration. My slated graduation date is late 2026.

The Power of Community

Throughout my journey, community was the thread that held me together. Counselors, pastors, family, mentors, and friends each played a vital role in my re-entry and success. Their support, encouragement, and belief in my potential made all the difference. Community is not just a safety net—it is a launching pad for dreams, healing, and achievement.

The Role of Mentors and Support Systems

Mrs. McNeil, the counselor who referred me to Mr. G's Diner, saw potential in me when I doubted myself. Mr. G, with his wisdom and kindness, reminded me daily that I was more than my past. Dr. Nicole B. Simpson provided spiritual guidance and a sense of belonging. My sisters sacrificed their own plans to ensure I had a place to come home to. Khayree offered love and companionship, helping me navigate the challenges of reentry.

Building New Connections

Community is built through relationships—big and small. The halfway house staff, college professors, coworkers, and church members all contributed to my growth. Each person played a role in helping me rebuild my life, offering support, encouragement, and opportunities.

Giving Back

As a public speaker and author, I use my story to empower others. I share my experiences to inspire hope and resilience, reminding others that they are not defined by their past. Community is about lifting each other up, sharing resources, and creating opportunities for growth.

Lessons Learned: Reflections on the Journey

- **Resilience:** Pain and adversity do not define your future. Every setback is an opportunity for growth.
- **Identity:** True freedom comes from reclaiming your identity and refusing to be limited by labels or numbers.
- **Faith:** Spiritual grounding and faith were essential in my healing and transformation.
- **Adaptability:** Life after incarceration required learning new skills and adapting to a rapidly changing world.
- **Purpose:** Motherhood, education, and career achievements gave me new reasons to strive and succeed.
- **Community:** The support of others is essential for healing, growth, and success.
- **Homeownership:** Becoming a homeowner was a milestone that marked my transition from instability to security, and it stands as a testament to perseverance and the power of community.

Conclusion: Breaking Down Walls

If you take nothing else from my story, know this: Life is what you make it. The hurt and pain of the past do not dictate your future. I chose to strip off the labels placed on me by society and others. I chose to dream, to heal, and to live up to my potential. With the support of a strong community, I am happy, I am free, and I am loved.

"A wall is just a wall, nothing more at all… it can be broken down." — Assata

FROM SURVIVAL TO SIGNIFICANCE

Building Legacy Through Community

Michael Middleton

Prologue: The Weight of Beginnings

I was born in the projects of Jersey City, where the rhythm of survival played louder than any lullaby. The streets were my first teachers, and their lessons were harsh, immediate, and unforgiving. In that world, success looked like hustling, fast money, and the kind of freedom that came with risk. I wasn't born bad—I was born into survival. The older cats on the block were my role models, and I followed their blueprint, believing it was the only way out.

But the streets have a way of calling you back, even when you swear you're done. My first arrest for possession and distribution of CDS was a wake-up call, but not enough to break the cycle. I went back, caught up in the same grind, until May 25th, 2005—when everything changed. Three years gone, most of it in a halfway house. Those years rewired my soul, forced me to confront the pain of separation, and made me question who I was and who I could become.

The Turning Point: Lessons Behind Walls

The hardest part of incarceration wasn't the walls—it was missing my family, the sound of familiar voices, the hugs that never came. That pain forced me to think differently, to ask myself what kind of man I wanted to be when I got home. The birth of my daughter while I was locked up was the deepest cut. I missed her first breath, her first cry, her tiny hand. That realization hit harder than any sentence. I knew I couldn't keep living recklessly. I had to become someone she could be proud of.

Inside, I found salvation in knowledge. I studied law in the prison library, reading cases, learning procedures, and filing motions. Understanding how power works became my new hustle. Even when the system broke me down, knowledge built me back up. I started seeing the system—and myself—differently.

But it wasn't just the law that saved me. Music and words had always been my way to breathe. Before prison, I recorded with Double X Posse—my man Brian Coleman, BK, a real one. (Rest in Peace, Brian.) We made music together, talked about life, and that creative bond lit a fire inside me that never left. In prison, my pen became my salvation. I wrote to stay free, even when my body wasn't. Those walls became my church, and writing became my way to redefine myself—not as a number, not as a statistic, but as a creator.

Reentry: Building Brick by Brick

When I came home in 2008, I brought a new plan—a redefined one. I started working at the Community Food Bank in Hillside, New Jersey. It wasn't glamorous, but it was honest. Then I drove limousines, learning patience, discipline, and the art of conversation. Each job was a brick in the foundation of my new life.

While in the halfway house, I joined Prodigal Sons and Daughters Redirectional Services, started by my brother and mentor Dennis Porter. That program changed my life—eight to twelve weeks of straight growth: financial literacy, conflict resolution, accountability. Conflict resolution stuck with me the most. I learned that life is energy—positive and negative bouncing off each other—and real peace comes from knowing how to balance it. I started living by a rule: every problem's got a solution, and sometimes you just have to agree to disagree to avoid being consumed by emotions during conflicts.

Achievements: Seeds of Purpose

Writing stayed with me wherever I went. During my first "bid," I started a manuscript that became my first self-published book, *Introduction to Hard 2 Da Kore*. It began as a movie script, but with my co-writer Kenyatta Williams, it grew into a full-length novel. That was the seed for my company, Hard 2 Da Kore Publications.

More books followed: *White Girl in a Black World* and *I Didn't Ask to Be Born... But Now That I'm Here*, subtitled *Changing Perspectives and Finding the Humanitarian Within*. These weren't just titles—they were testimonies, reflections of my personal growth, pain, redemption, and purpose.

Somewhere down the road, I reconnected with Dr. Nicole B. Simpson, who grew up in the same hood. She invited me to join her Dare 2 Dream Institute, where I took her "You Are a Business" course. On or around July 15th, 2021, I received my certificate and a new mindset. Her course made me see myself as a brand—not just a writer or artist, but a business. With her guidance, I started One Family Productions LLC. My mentality shifted for good. I wasn't just creating art—I was creating value within my art.

I kept moving—writing, publishing, building. I'm currently working on *Hard 2 Da Kore 2: The Ghost Rydrz*, a *White Girl in a Black World* spinoff titled *Boy Toys for Hire*, and a seven-volume series called *I Didn't Ask to Be Born Again... But Now That I'm Here*. Each project is another piece of my purpose.

Then I branched out. I built Michael Middleton Consulting LLC, formed a C-Corp (M2 Capital Holdings, Inc.), started a DBA (M2 Mortgage Group), stepped into real estate, bought a few lots, and learned the business side of ownership. Now I'm not chasing fast money—I'm building lasting money. Legacy money. The kind my daughter can stand on one day.

Lessons Learned: Growth Through Loss and Love

Since I've been home, life has tested me again and again. I lost my mother in 2014 and my younger sister in 2020. Losing them shook me, made me question life and death, and forced me to search for meaning. I started studying spirituality, reading, exploring, and trying to understand what happens when we leave this world. In 2018, I dove deep into metaphysics, constitutional law, trust law, business law—anything that could teach me how to stand on my rights and understand the bigger picture.

True freedom isn't just about open doors or the absence of physical barriers—it's about the state of your mind and spirit. There were days when I walked the streets, technically "free," but felt trapped by fear, anger, or the weight of expectations. And there were nights behind locked doors when my thoughts soared, unbound by circumstance. That's when I realized: the most powerful prisons are invisible, built from doubt, regret, or unresolved pain.

Freedom, I discovered, is a practice. It's waking up and choosing not to be defined by your past, your mistakes, or the labels others put on you. It's learning to let go of grudges, to forgive yourself and others, and to move forward with intention. The world outside is always shifting—new technologies, changing systems, evolving beliefs. If you cling to old ways, you risk becoming a relic, stuck in a moment that no longer exists.

So I made a commitment to myself: keep learning, keep growing, keep adapting. I read books that challenged my thinking, sought out mentors who pushed me beyond my comfort zone, and surrounded myself with people who inspired me to be better. Patience became my anchor. Emotional control became my shield. Balance became my goal.

Protecting my peace is an everyday discipline. It means setting boundaries, saying no to negativity, and refusing to let anyone else dictate my worth. It means finding stillness in chaos, clarity in confusion, and hope in hardship.

Sometimes, the greatest act of freedom is simply choosing to be at peace with yourself, no matter what's happening around you.

In the end, being free is about living authentically—embracing your journey, honoring your growth, and believing in your ability to change. It's about understanding that while the world may try to lock you up in its expectations, you hold the key to your own liberation

I practice staying at zero point—not letting negativity lower my vibration. If someone throws shade, I send love. If someone doubts me, I let my actions speak louder. Sometimes I go back to that stillness I found inside those walls—not out of pain, but out of peace. Stillness gives clarity, and clarity keeps me grounded.

The Power of Community: Building Together

None of this happened alone. Every achievement, every lesson, every step forward was made possible by the community around me. From the mentors who guided me, to the friends who believed in me, to the family who loved me even when I couldn't love myself—community was the foundation.

Programs like Prodigal Sons and Daughters, Redirectional Services, and Dare 2 Dream Institute didn't just teach skills—they built networks of support. They showed me that real change happens when people come together, share knowledge, and lift each other up. My businesses, my books, my growth—they're all rooted in the soil of community.

Community is more than a group of people—it's a force. It's the energy that turns pain into purpose, struggle into strength, and dreams into reality. When I look at my daughter, I see the legacy I'm building—not just for her, but for everyone who comes after. Legacy isn't about money or fame—it's about impact. It's about leaving the world better than you found it, and that only happens when you build together.

Conclusion: From the Core to the Calling

Transformation is rarely a straight line. It's a winding path, marked by setbacks, revelations, and the quiet moments when you realize you're not the same person you once were. For me, the journey began in the chaos of the projects, where survival was the only currency and trust was earned in small, hard-won increments. The streets shaped my instincts—taught me to read people, to sense danger, to move with caution and confidence. That awareness became my armor, but it also became a lens through which I saw the world: sharp, unfiltered, and sometimes unforgiving.

Prison was a crucible. It stripped away the distractions and forced me to confront myself—my choices, my regrets, my hopes. Patience wasn't just a virtue; it was a necessity. Days blurred into weeks, and weeks into years, but in that stillness, I learned to listen. I listened to the stories of others, to the wisdom tucked inside old law books, to the rhythm of my own heartbeat as I wrote page after page. Patience taught me that growth is slow, that healing takes time, and that redemption is possible if you're willing to do the work.

Love, when it finally found me, was both a balm and a challenge. It demanded vulnerability, forgiveness, and the courage to let go of old wounds. Love showed me that transformation isn't just about changing your circumstances—it's about changing your heart. It's about learning to accept yourself, flaws and all, and to extend that acceptance to others. Love taught me that we are all works in progress, and that grace is the bridge between who we were and who we can become.

Purpose is the compass that guides me now. It's the reason I get up each morning, the fuel behind every project, every book, every business venture. Purpose makes struggles meaningful, turns pain into strength, and converts setbacks into progress. It's not just about personal success—it's about creating something that lasts, something that lifts others as it lifts me.

But none of this happened in isolation. Transformation is a collective act. It's the mentors who offered guidance, the friends who believed in me, the family who stood by me even when I faltered. It's the community programs that provided tools and support, the creative collaborators who sparked new ideas, the readers who found hope in my words. Every person who played a part in my journey is a note in the symphony of my transformation.

In the end, transformation is about becoming more than you imagined possible—not just for yourself, but for everyone whose life you touch. It's about turning survival into significance, and pain into purpose, through the power of connection and community.

I'm still writing. Still building. Still walking in truth. Still living my purpose—one day at a time, one minute at a time, one second at a time. The lessons I've learned—about resilience, growth, and the strength of community—are the foundation of everything I do.

If there's one thing I know for sure, it's this: we rise by lifting others. The power of a strong community isn't just in what it gives you—it's in what it allows you to give back. Legacy is built together, and together, we can turn survival into significance.

Three of the founders of the Generation X Community Association. Sonji K. Grandy, Dr. Nicole B. Simpson, & Jesse L. Simpson III.

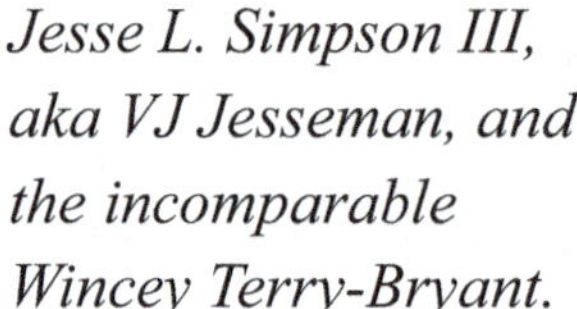

Jesse L. Simpson III, aka VJ Jesseman, and the incomparable Wincey Terry-Bryant.

The Generation X team is hard at work at The Gospelfest in 2009.

Generation NEXT... The founders' beautiful daughters, Emani B. Simpson and Tyniece S. Bradley-Gutzmore, have grown into amazingly accomplished young women. Emani is an actress, writer, director, and producer, and Tyniece is a fashion designer, stylist, minister, and award-winning author.

Rev. Dr. Lewis Dixon, Sonji & Dr. Nicole are representing in South Jersey at one of the many toy drives sponsored by Generation X.

In the 90's and 2000's Dr. Nicole was a prominent television personality both locally and nationally via the Power of Gospel television and radio program.

The board of Generation X has awarded a scholarship to one of the many recipients over the years.

Kayla Smith, recipient of the Dare 2 Dream scholarship, has gone on to do tremendous things with the help of Generation X.

Another worthy scholarship recipient was presented with a check from the Generation X board members.

Sonji and the fourth founding member of Generation X, Sherri Hedgeman.

Sonji and Dr. Nicole have hosted numerous impactful seminars through their Wealth Protection and Management initiative. Their goal is to see families secured financially for future generations.

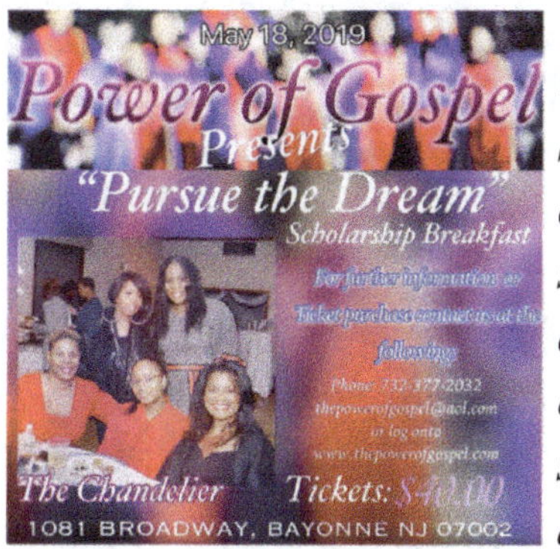

The Pursue the Dream Scholarship Breakfast was created to celebrate and support the academic pursuits of high school graduates entering college. Nearly 100 scholarships have been awarded to deserving students.

The joy and smile of a child is always the goal of Generation X, not just for the holiday, but every day.

Dr. Nicole is serving at one of the many highly anticipated toy drives.

More smiling faces at the Generation X toy drive.

Board member Mitchell Y. Slade showing off the sought after Gift card apron, a fundraiser given annually to raise money for Generation X.

Sonji awarding the winner of the gift card apron with her prize.

One of the many amazing families touched by the work of Generation X.

The bike giveaway has been a staple of the Generation X toy drive from the beginning. Hundreds of bikes have been awarded to deserving children across New Jersey.

Dr. Nicole is attending one of the many events honoring and recognizing Generation X's contributions to the community.

Beloved Dare 2 Dream Institute instructor and creative director Professor Kay Lindsay is speaking to the graduates and their families at graduation.

Dare 2 Dream Institute graduate Jasmine Wilkes.

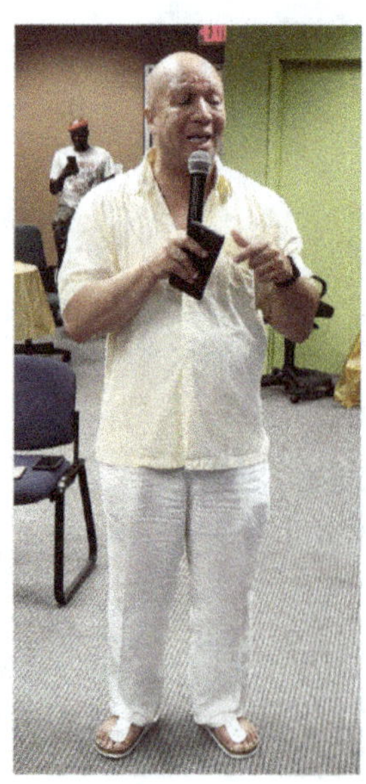

Dynamic keynote speaker and instructor, Dr. DeLacy Davis, spoke life to the graduates at the Dare 2 Dream Institute graduation.

THE JOURNEY BACK TO SAFETY

Shavon Price

Introduction

Reentry after incarceration is a journey few truly understand. The world expects you to pick up where you left off, but the reality is a landscape of invisible barriers, emotional hurdles, and a persistent sense of loss. My journey back to safety has been shaped by setbacks, achievements, and—most importantly—lessons that continue to guide me. This chapter is my attempt to share those lessons, in the hope that others navigating similar paths will find validation, insight, and perhaps a measure of hope.

The Weight of Lost Time

The hardest thing about life after prison is the quiet grief—the FOMO, the "fear of missing out"—that lingers long after release. Years of my life were taken, and no amount of freedom can return them. You are expected to rebuild from what remains, to create a "new normal" while living under an undercurrent of restrictions. Some are real. Some are assumed. Most are hella permanent. Yes, consequences are a result of your actions, but punishment isn't meant to be perpetual. Post-prison, you have to actively reject that feeling in your body—the perpetual "No" that follows you around, making you brace for it in every conversation. You rehearse it. Prepare to handle it better and better. It's almost like taking a punch.

Navigating Restriction and Rebuilding

When I left prison, I was given a choice: a halfway house or New Jersey's Intensive Supervision Program (ISP). My family was suffering from my absence, so I chose ISP, hoping to be closer to them. I quickly learned that ISP was not freedom—it was another kind of prison. The rules were exhaustive: no gifts without approval, curfews, mandatory employment, restitution payments that took a quarter of my income, and constant check-ins. I followed every rule, determined to prove I was "rehabilitated." On paper, I was a model participant. Inside, I was struggling. I excelled at every task, but I was empty, fighting to prove my worth to a society that seemed determined to keep me in a box.

I wanted freedom so badly that I traded it for another prison. My mental health was struggling, yet I was constantly excelling. Everything life put in front of me, I excelled at. I followed the playbook. I was a good person, so why was I miserable? I didn't suffer in silence, though. I excelled AND cried out loud. I fought hard for myself. I became involved in every program and did everything they said. On paper, I was a model rehabilitated prisoner, but inside, I was empty. I was destroying myself. Fighting against society to prove that I deserved to be there.

Achievements and Setbacks

Eight years after my release, I was thriving by many measures. I worked for a Fortune 500 company, studied artificial intelligence, and was selected for an executive assistant role at an agricultural technology firm working on important projects in East Africa. I was excited—not just for the job, but for the chance to matter, to be seen for who I had become. But my past followed me. The offer was rescinded after a background check revealed my record, and I was denied the government security clearance required for the role. It didn't matter how hard I had worked or how much I had changed. My résumé was overshadowed by a piece of paper from my past.

This wasn't the first time. Over the years, I lost twelve job offers, was denied entry to countries, and even turned away from volunteer opportunities. Each "no" was a reminder that, for many, punishment is perpetual. Yet, I kept moving forward. Between 2019 and 2022, I received a $30,000 raise and a promotion, traveled the world, and built two businesses while working full-time. Outwardly, I was successful. Inwardly, I was battling depression and the echo of rejection.

The Impact of Community

Family support influenced my choices, and professional networks opened doors. At the same time, broader society often imposed barriers—through policies, stigma, and exclusion that shaped what was possible and what was not. Healing, for me, came through building new communities when familiar ones fell away.

When I found the Dare 2 Dream Institute, Sonji L. Grandy truly saw me. She was the first person to recognize not only where I was, but also the kind of support I needed to move forward. She became both a mentor and a friend. Despite my guardedness and lingering bitterness, Sonji met me with patience, love, and a willingness to listen. She was one of the first people to ask me not who I had been, but who I was becoming.

When she sensed the depth of my sadness, she flew to Georgia to see me. She met me exactly where I was and gently encouraged me to see myself the way others already did—as someone worthy of a full, expansive life. Sonji became the launching pad I needed. She taught me to honor my own pace, to listen for my own voice, and to trust again. Most importantly, she gave me what I needed to move on: the courage to share my story.

Lessons Learned

1. Resilience Is a Practice, Not a Trait

Resilience is often described as something you have or don't have, but my experience taught me it's a skill you build, day by day, through conscious effort. Every "no"—from job offers rescinded to opportunities denied—forced me to confront my own worth. I learned that resilience wasn't just about enduring hardship, but about redefining myself beyond my record. I had to persist, adapt, and keep moving, even when the world said I didn't belong.

There were days when the weight of rejection felt unbearable. I remember sitting in my car after losing yet another job offer, feeling the familiar sting of shame and frustration. But I also remember the small victories: the first time I advocated for myself in a professional setting, the first time I shared my story publicly, the first time I realized that my value was not determined by a background check. Each of these moments was a brick in the foundation of my resilience.

I also learned that resilience is not a solitary pursuit. It's built in community, in the quiet encouragement of friends and family, in the shared stories of others who have walked similar paths. I found strength in the knowledge that I was not alone, that my struggles were part of a larger narrative of survival and transformation.

2. Productivity Without Compassion Is Punishment

For years, I measured my value by output and compliance. I believed that if I worked hard enough, followed every rule, and exceeded every expectation, I would finally be accepted. But true progress came when I realized that productivity must honor humanity. I stopped performing for others' comfort and started embracing authenticity, even when it made people uncomfortable.

This lesson was hard-won. I spent years burning out, pushing myself to the brink in pursuit of external validation. I took on extra projects, volunteered for every committee, and worked late into the night, all in the hope that someone would see my worth. But the more I achieved, the emptier I felt. It wasn't until I began to practice self-compassion—allowing myself to rest, to make mistakes, to be imperfect—that I started to heal.

In my consulting work, I now emphasize the importance of compassionate systems. I help organizations design workflows that prioritize well-being, not just efficiency. I encourage leaders to recognize the humanity of their teams, to create spaces where people can bring their whole selves to work.

Productivity, I've learned, is most sustainable when it is rooted in care for ourselves and for each other.

3. Authenticity Is Liberating

The pressure to perform gratitude and humility for acceptance was unsustainable. My anger became my liberation. I stopped performing "goodness" and started telling the truth about my experience. Honesty was turbulent, but it was necessary for healing and growth.

There is a unique exhaustion that comes from constantly editing yourself to fit others' expectations. For years, I felt compelled to downplay my struggles, to present a sanitized version of my story that would be palatable to employers, colleagues, and even friends. But this performance took a toll on my mental health. I became disconnected from my own emotions, unsure of where the mask ended and I began.

The turning point came when I started sharing my story openly—first in small circles, then on social media, and eventually in professional settings. I spoke about the realities of reentry, the pain of rejection, and the ongoing process of healing. The response was overwhelming. People reached out to share their own stories, to thank me for my honesty, to tell me that my vulnerability had given them permission to be more authentic themselves.

Authenticity, I discovered, is contagious. It creates space for others to show up as they are, to share their own truths, to build deeper connections. It is not always easy, and it often comes with risk, but it is the foundation of genuine community and lasting change.

4. Community Is Both Barrier and Lifeline

Family support influenced my choices, and professional networks opened doors. Broader society often imposed barriers—through policies, stigma, and exclusion. Yet, I found healing in building new communities. I founded SYS Consulting US, a firm that helps people and organizations design systems that support real life, not just productivity. Sharing my journey and insights on social media connected me with others rebuilding after trauma. These communities have been essential to my ongoing integration and self-acceptance.

Community, I've learned, is not a monolith. It can be both a source of pain and a wellspring of hope. There were times when I felt isolated by the very people who were supposed to support me—when friends distanced themselves, when colleagues whispered behind my back, when institutions closed their doors. But there were also moments of profound connection: the friend who showed up with groceries when I couldn't afford to eat, the mentor who advocated for me in a boardroom, the stranger who sent a message of encouragement after reading my story online.

Building community requires vulnerability and persistence. It means reaching out, even when you fear rejection. It means creating spaces where others feel seen and valued. Through SYS Consulting US, I have had the privilege of helping others build supportive networks—whether through peer support groups, professional associations, or online communities. These connections are not just a safety net; they are a launching pad for growth and transformation.

5. Healing Is Ongoing and Nonlinear

Today, I am not "healed" or "finished," but I am integrated. My business reflects who I am, not who I was trained to be. Rebuilding is possible. It's not about becoming someone new—it's about building a life and a business that can hold who you already are. Community, authenticity, and compassion are the foundations of true rehabilitation. We all deserve the chance to fill the void left by trauma and to be welcomed back with open arms.

Healing, I've discovered, is not a destination but a journey. There are days when I feel strong and confident, and days when old wounds resurface. I have learned to be gentle with myself, to recognize that setbacks are part of the process. I have developed rituals—yoga, journaling, creative hobbies—that help me stay grounded. I have sought therapy, leaned on friends, and allowed myself to grieve what was lost.

In my work, I encourage others to embrace the messiness of healing. I remind clients that progress is rarely linear, that growth often comes in fits and starts. I celebrate small victories and honor the courage it takes to keep moving forward. Healing is not about erasing the past; it is about integrating it into a richer, more complex sense of self.

Moving Forward

Now that you've heard me scream into the void, what have I been doing? Honestly, I have been recalibrating but also working. Today, I run SYS Consulting US, a systems and operations consulting firm that helps people and organizations build structures that actually support how they live and work. I help founders, executives, and teams identify where their time, energy, and resources are leaking, then design practical systems that restore clarity, sustainability, and trust in themselves. At its core, my work is about helping people stop performing productivity and start living inside systems that make sense. One of my core clients is a twenty-year-old beverage company, which is now located in 18 stores across the Southeast, including Whole Foods, The Fresh Market, and Robert Fresh.

This version of my business didn't happen overnight. It is the result of a two-year identity shift that began after I wrote my book, *Repairing Time Leaks*, which was facilitated by the Dare to Dream Institute. At the time, I believed my philosophies around productivity were about discipline, structure, and optimization. What I understand now is that many of those beliefs were rooted in my own Good Person Handbook, the idea that worthiness comes from output, compliance, and constant improvement. As I began studying my own patterns more honestly, I realized that productivity without compassion is just another form of punishment. That realization changed everything.

I began to slow down. I returned to my body through yoga. I returned to my art through craft, analog hobbies, and making things without an agenda. I stopped trying to master myself the way institutions had once tried to manage me, and instead became my own guru. I started studying myself with the same curiosity and rigor that others had always applied to me. In doing so, my work evolved. SYS Consulting US is no longer about forcing efficiency; it is about designing systems that honor capacity, humanity, and truth.

I also share ongoing reflections and practical insights about systems for everyday life on Instagram @sysconsultingus. This is a newer concept but the ideas are rooted in real life that often translate directly into business for solo entrepreneurs. If you want to see the quieter side of my integration, you can find me on TikTok @MaudesPlaceCo, where I share my analog hobbies, yoga practice, and the slower rituals that help me stay connected to myself.

This work is not about becoming someone new. It's about building a life and a business that can hold who you already are.

Conclusion

My journey back to safety is a testament to the power of resilience, compassion, authenticity, and community. These lessons have shaped not only my career but my sense of self. If my story resonates with you, know that you are not alone—and that rebuilding is possible, one lesson at a time.

WALKING IN FREEDOM

A Journey of Grace, Growth, and Community

Tiyanna Scarlett

Introduction: From Brokenness to Purpose

My life is a living testimony of grace, growth, and redemption. There was a time when I didn't believe those words could ever apply to me. I once moved through life broken, numb, and unsure if I would ever find purpose again. But today, I can stand firmly and say that I am walking in freedom—not just the kind that opens prison doors, but the kind that opens the heart. My journey since incarceration has been one of pain, healing, discovery, and transformation. Every step has taught me that redemption is not a single moment, but a process of becoming.

The Weight of Reentry and the Stigma of Incarceration

When I came home, I was determined that my past would not be the full story of who I was. I carried the weight of shame and guilt, but I also carried the quiet hope that maybe God wasn't done with me yet. However, that hope did not become my starting point, and for me, reentry was not easy. I was still lost and afraid of who I thought I was. I was suffocated by shame and guilt, not understanding trauma and its effects. The world moved fast, and the stigma of incarceration lingers even after the sentence is complete.

For the first few years of my release, I mentally reincarcerated myself without realizing it, and I suffered greatly from it. I isolated myself by going to Atlantic City, a land with no milk and honey. No resources for those who are trauma-impacted. Just a strip of opportunity to feed one's greed and fast life desires. I won't lie, I was stuck. But then help came. And, while I lacked confidence at that time, I refused to let my past dictate my future. I began rebuilding piece by piece, trusting the people and tools God had provided.

I internalized the mindset that if God could restore my peace, He could restore my path.

Education: The Bridge to Identity and Achievement

One of the most defining parts of my journey was education. While I was still incarcerated, I was introduced to the NJ-STEP program, and that experience completely changed the way I saw myself. For years, I had believed the lie that I was not smart enough or capable enough to achieve anything meaningful. But the first time I sat in a college classroom, surrounded by women who were determined to learn despite their circumstances, something awakened in me.

Higher education gave me language for my pain and power for my purpose. It became the foundation that helped me think critically, communicate clearly, and believe in the value of my contributions to the world. Through NJ-STEP, I first earned my associate's degree, and even after leaving prison, I remained an active part of the STEP community. By 2024, I walked across the stage at Rutgers University, graduating with my Master of Social Work, still connected to the NJ-STEP network that had nurtured me from the start. I walked across that stage with dignity, having earned not only my MSW but, most importantly, my self-respect.

Those years of schooling taught me that education has the power to rebuild identity. It's not just about earning a diploma. It's about reimagining who you are and what you deserve. For people who have faced incarceration, access to education is often the bridge between survival and success. It teaches discipline, structure, and hope. I saw women who came from broken systems start to believe again. And for me, it wasn't just about grades, it was about purpose. Education taught me that I could take the same determination that once kept me alive in dark places and use it to build a meaningful future. It became part of my ministry, showing others that knowledge is not limited by walls.

Personal Growth: Motherhood, Advocacy, and Resilience

After coming home, besides my setbacks, my hunger for growth didn't stop. I continued pursuing higher education while learning how to navigate life. Through those years, I became a wife and a mother. That journey was short-lived, though, because after a few years of an unhealthy marriage, I also became a divorced mother, co-parenting a beautiful four-year-old boy who is nonverbal and autistic. This part of my life has not been the easiest. To be honest, it has been one of the hardest, most humbling challenges of my life. Every moment requires patience, advocacy, and unwavering love.

Motherhood has taught me grace, resilience, and the profound responsibility of shaping a life that depends on me, and through it all, I continue to grow alongside him. My son is my heartbeat, the reason I push forward on days when I feel weary. Being his mother has taught me patience, advocacy, and unconditional love. Through him I've learned to slow down, celebrate progress rather than perfection, and find joy in the smallest victories: every new word, every smile, every moment of connection. Just as I once fought for my own freedom, I now fight for his future. Through this journey, I have discovered a strength I didn't know I possessed. Messiah has shown me the true meaning of love, connection, and sacrifice, and he continually reminds me why every effort, every struggle, and every act of devotion is worth it.

Professional Achievements: Clinician and Healer

Becoming a clinician was not something I stumbled into. It was a calling. I first came home working with individuals with physical, mental, and intellectual disabilities—the Division of Developmental Disabilities population. Then, as I journeyed through school, majoring in Social Work, I worked in yet another vulnerable population: Substance. I realized I had a niche for healing those who were vulnerable. Now my life allows me to walk alongside others who are fighting to rebuild their lives. Every session, every story, every breakthrough reminds me that healing is possible. I've learned that people don't need to be fixed; they need to be understood, affirmed, and reminded that they are not their worst decisions. The same compassion I extend to my clients is the compassion that once saved me.

There are moments of exhaustion and frustration, days when the world feels overwhelming, and nights when I question if I'm doing enough. Yet, in the midst of the struggle, I've discovered depths of strength I never knew I had. The lessons I have learned through my clinical work mirror the lessons I have learned in my personal healing. I have learned that change requires consistency, humility, and faith. I have learned that growth hurts sometimes, but that pain is often the evidence of something new being born. I have learned that accountability is not punishment, but it's freedom. Most importantly, I have learned that every experience, even the painful ones, can be used for God's glory if you allow Him to rewrite the narrative.

Rediscovering Love and Spiritual Foundation

One of the greatest gifts of my journey has been rediscovering love. For a long time, I was truly afraid to open my heart again. I had been through too much, and trust didn't come easily. Every broken promise, every disappointment, every moment of doubt had left me cautious, guarding my heart as if it were fragile glass. But through prayer, therapy, and the gentle guidance of my church leaders, I began to see that love is not meant to hurt or confine. It's meant to heal, affirm, and strengthen. Love came into my life during a season when I was learning to see myself differently, learning that I am worthy, capable, and deserving of care and respect. Its presence has been steady, patient, and kind, offering reassurance in moments of uncertainty and encouragement when I doubted myself.

None of this transformation would have been possible without my spiritual foundation. Micah 7 Ministries is not just my church. It's my home, my refuge, my house of hope. My pastor, Dr. Rev. Nicole B. Simpson, has been both a spiritual mother and a living example of what grace in leadership looks like. She believed in me when I didn't believe in myself. She saw beyond my past and spoke to my potential. Under her guidance, I have learned how to serve with humility, lead with compassion, and trust God with my process. Every sermon, every prayer, every hug from a member of our church family has been part of my healing.

Minister Sonji, my mentor, has been another divine gift. Her guidance has been patient, purposeful, and deeply rooted in love. She walks with me, not ahead of me, reminding me that progress is not about speed, but about direction. Through her, I have learned that mentorship is sacred. It is where wisdom meets accountability. Her presence in my life has strengthened my faith and sharpened my character. When I falter, she reminds me who I am and whose I am.

The Power of Community: Lessons Learned

At Micah 7, we often say that we are a family of believers who love beyond the walls. Every member plays a vital role in my life. I have witnessed what community truly looks like—people who show up, pray with you, celebrate you, and remind you of your worth. It is in that house of hope where I have learned to forgive myself fully and to give God my yes without fear. The church has been my training ground for purpose. It is where I learned that leadership is service, and service is love in action. My church community has stood with me through every storm, and I am thriving today because they helped me see that I was never alone.

Reflecting on my journey, I realize that freedom means so much more than being released from a physical place. True freedom is mental, emotional, and spiritual. It is learning to let go of shame and to embrace the lessons that pain taught you. I used to think my mistakes disqualified me from purpose, but I have learned that God specializes in using the broken to build something beautiful. My past became the soil for my purpose. My pain became my platform. And my testimony became a tool to empower others who are still trying to find their way.

I have also learned the importance of boundaries, self-worth, and balance. Healing requires intentional work. I have had to learn how to say no, how to rest, and how to forgive myself for what I did not know before I knew better. I have learned that humility does not mean shrinking; it means standing confidently in who God says you are while staying teachable. I take pride in the woman I am today because I know what it took to become her. Every degree, every certification, every client I help, every obstacle I have overcome—it all stands as evidence of God's restoration.

Conclusion: The Transformative Power of Community

As a clinician, I now understand that purpose often grows out of pain. I use my experiences to connect with others who feel unseen. I show up as proof that redemption is possible. I hold space for people to feel safe, to cry, to grow, to hope again. There is no greater honor than using what once broke you to help someone else heal. My story reminds me daily that transformation is not about perfection; it is about perseverance.

In this current season of my life, I am thriving, healing, trusting God, and walking boldly in my purpose. I no longer view my past as a place of shame, but as a part of my testimony. I see every chapter before, during, and after incarceration as necessary. Without those valleys, I would not understand the mountaintop moments. Without those dark nights, I would not appreciate the light I now live in. I am a mother, a clinician, a believer, a partner, and a woman who knows her worth. I am proud of myself, not because everything is perfect, but because I have learned how to keep going with grace.

The greatest lesson I have learned along the way is that God's grace is not just for the worthy; it is for the willing. I was willing to be taught, willing to heal, and willing to surrender. And while I am still learning, I am willing. Through that willingness, my life has become a living reflection of what happens when faith meets action. I have learned that success is not about titles or recognition. It is about transformation. About being able to look back at the woman I was and smile, knowing I did not give up when I could have.

Today, I wake up with purpose. I counsel others with empathy. I love with depth. I mother my son with patience. And I serve with gratitude. Every part of my life now carries meaning. I am not defined by what I lost, but by what I have gained: peace, wisdom, strength, and an unshakable faith. I am still evolving, but I am proud of who I am becoming. My story is proof that redemption is real, that healing is possible, and that hope is stronger than any prison wall. And if there's one thing I know for sure, it is that I am exactly where God needs me to be.

DARE TO DREAM

From Shadows to Light

Vincent McDonald

I. Roots and Reckoning

I was born in Hillside, a small suburban town nestled among the bustling cities of Newark, Irvington, and Elizabeth. My family was my first community—a tapestry of love, support, and tradition. My parents, high school sweethearts, married before I was born, and I was the second and last child. Our home was filled with warmth, laughter, and the kind of encouragement that shapes a person's earliest dreams.

Yet, as adolescence crept in, so did the allure of the streets. The "freedom" I saw in street life was intoxicating—a counterculture that rejected the system and promised belonging. Gang culture, especially in New Jersey during the late 90s and early 2000s, was everywhere: in music, fashion, and the very fabric of urban life. Businesses capitalized on this movement, selling merchandise that made the lifestyle visible and desirable. I pledged my affiliation, drawn by the promise of family and the thrill of criminality.

Despite my loving upbringing, I developed an edge that led me down a dangerous path. Small crimes escalated into riskier ventures, and eventually, I was arrested and convicted for multiple robberies across New Jersey. My sentence: fifteen years, with a mandatory 85% to be served behind bars. Prison became my new reality, and the trajectory of my life seemed set.

II. Transformation Behind Walls

At twenty-three, facing a fifteen-year sentence, I was forced to confront the future. Every emotion—fear, regret, anger, hope—washed over me. I had to decide what kind of life I wanted if I survived this ordeal.

Prison was a crucible. I joined a meditation group that met on Mondays, learning centering prayer and the art of self-reflection. I rebuilt myself from the inside out, focusing on my relationship with God and the values my family had instilled in me. I became an avid reader, devouring books on business, investing, and even science fiction. My intellectual curiosity expanded, and I found solace in learning.

Family remained my anchor. Their prayers and support kept me focused, reminding me that I was not meant to pass on a legacy of failure. Education became my lifeline. I attended college and graduated from various certificate and degree programs while incarcerated. Each achievement was a step toward redemption, a testament to my determination to grow. My relationship with God deepened, providing strength through the darkest times.

III. Reentry and Renewal

Upon release, I faced a world that had changed—and so had I. My plan was simple: go back to school. I enrolled at Rutgers University for my sophomore year, determined to complete my bachelor's degree in three years. At thirty-six, I was a student at Rutgers Business School in Newark, NJ, returning home to a twelve-year-old daughter and a catalog of unpublished manuscripts.

I dared to dream. My goal was to start my own business, using the skills I had honed during my time away. The Dare to Dream Institute became my launching pad, giving me an outlet to express myself and pursue my passion for publishing. I read extensively about self-publishing, learning the legalities and intricacies of the industry. My catalog grew, especially in Urban Fantasy.

Mentorship played a pivotal role in my journey, with Dr. Nicole envisioning not just a publishing company but a media empire for me, and Sonji Grandy guiding me through the process of publishing two books within seven days. The transformative support I received reinforced my belief in the power of community, and the continued encouragement from Sonji Grandy over the next year helped me maintain momentum in both my business and personal life. I am deeply grateful to have met someone who wanted nothing in return except my commitment to pursuing my own goals and dreams. Through weekly phone calls, Sonji Grandy helped me evaluate and reflect on my progress, encouraging me to pause and appreciate how far I had come rather than rushing to the next milestone. Her advice enabled me to achieve sustainable growth and success, balancing ambition with gratitude and self-care.

I started a podcast for entrepreneurs, an organic extension of my journey. Sharing my story and insights, I connected with others who were navigating similar paths. The podcast became a platform for encouragement and education, amplifying the voices of those who dared to dream.

IV. Building Businesses and Breaking Barriers

My entrepreneurial spirit led me to the Profeta Foundation's ten-week program for aspiring business owners. Every Saturday, I learned essential skills—from crafting business plans to presenting to investors. My second business idea, property preservation and management, took shape through research and mentorship. At the program's conclusion, I presented my plan and received enthusiastic support, a confidence boost that propelled me forward.

RU-Flourishing, a nonprofit supporting formerly incarcerated entrepreneurs, offered another opportunity. I competed for grant funding, presenting my business and winning one of four grants. This recognition was more than financial—it was validation of my journey and a testament to the resilience of those who refuse to be defined by their past.

I continued to build my business, encouraging young entrepreneurs and formerly incarcerated individuals to invest in themselves. My story became a beacon, illuminating the path for others who faced similar obstacles.

V. Achievements

Academic Success

Earning multiple certificates and degrees while incarcerated was a monumental achievement. It required discipline, focus, and a willingness to embrace change. Education opened doors, providing the knowledge and confidence needed to pursue new opportunities.

Entrepreneurial Triumphs

Launching two businesses—one in publishing and one in property management—demonstrated the power of vision and perseverance. Winning grant funding and successfully presenting to investors were milestones that affirmed my capabilities and potential.

Creative Expression

Publishing manuscripts and starting a podcast allowed me to share my story and insights with a broader audience. Creativity became a tool for healing and empowerment, fostering connection and understanding.

Personal Growth

The journey from incarceration to entrepreneurship was marked by profound personal growth. I learned the importance of self-reflection, resilience, and faith. Each setback became a lesson, each achievement a stepping-stone toward a brighter future.

VI. Lessons Learned from Setbacks

Setbacks have a way of shaping us in ways that success alone cannot. My journey—from the streets of Hillside to prison, and then to entrepreneurship—was marked by moments of failure, disappointment, and loss. Each setback was a crossroads, forcing me to choose between surrender and resilience.

The Power of Self-Reflection

My first major setback was my incarceration. The abrupt loss of freedom was devastating. I had to confront the reality of my choices and the pain I had caused my family. In those early days behind bars, anger and regret threatened to consume me. But prison also stripped away distractions, leaving me alone with my thoughts. I learned that self-reflection is not just a tool for understanding the past—it is essential for shaping the future. Through meditation and centering prayer, I began to see my life with clarity. I realized that my actions did not define my worth, and that change was possible if I was willing to do the work.

Embracing Vulnerability

Setbacks exposed my vulnerabilities. The birth of my daughter while I was incarcerated was bittersweet—I could not hold her until she was three years old. The pain of missing her early years was a constant reminder of what I had lost. Yet, this vulnerability became a source of strength. It motivated me to become a better father, to rebuild trust, and to create a future where she could be proud of me. I learned that acknowledging pain is not a sign of weakness; it is the first step toward healing.

The Importance of Adaptability

Prison life demanded adaptability. The environment was unpredictable, and survival required flexibility. I learned to navigate complex social dynamics, to find opportunities for growth even in restrictive circumstances. When my initial attempts at self-improvement were met with skepticism or resistance, I adapted my approach—seeking out new mentors, exploring different educational programs, and remaining open to change. Adaptability became a cornerstone of my resilience, preparing me for the challenges I would face after release.

Turning Failure into Fuel

Not every plan succeeded. There were times when I failed exams, missed opportunities, or faced rejection from programs and organizations. Each failure stung, but I refused to let it define me. Instead, I treated failure as feedback—a signal to adjust my strategy, work harder, or seek help. This mindset shift was transformative. I learned to celebrate small victories and to view setbacks as stepping-stones rather than stumbling blocks.

The Value of Perseverance

Perseverance was tested daily. The process of earning degrees and certificates while incarcerated was grueling. There were moments when I wanted to give up, when the weight of my sentence felt unbearable. But I kept going, driven by the belief that every effort brought me closer to redemption. Perseverance taught me that progress is often slow and incremental, but consistency yields results. This lesson carried over into my entrepreneurial ventures, where setbacks were inevitable, but persistence paid off.

Seeking and Accepting Help

One of the hardest lessons was learning to ask for help. Pride and shame made it difficult to reach out, especially when I felt I had let others down. But community—family, mentors, and organizations—became my lifeline. Their support reminded me that setbacks are not meant to be faced alone. Accepting help required humility, but it also opened doors to new opportunities and resources. I learned that strength is found in collaboration, and that community amplifies resilience.

Reframing the Narrative

Society often stigmatizes those who have been incarcerated, viewing setbacks as permanent marks of failure. I learned to reframe my narrative, to see my past not as a liability but as a source of wisdom and empathy.

Sharing my story through writing and podcasting allowed me to connect with others who faced similar challenges. I discovered that vulnerability and authenticity inspire trust, and that my setbacks could serve as a beacon for others seeking hope.

Building Resilience Through Faith

Faith was a constant companion. In moments of despair, prayer and spiritual reflection provided comfort and guidance. I learned that setbacks are opportunities to deepen faith, to trust in a purpose greater than myself. Faith gave me the courage to dream again, to believe in the possibility of transformation even when the odds seemed insurmountable.

The Role of Community in Overcoming Setbacks

Every lesson learned from adversity was magnified by the presence of a strong community. Family, mentors, and organizations like Dare to Dream Foundation and RU-Flourishing provided encouragement, resources, and accountability. Community transformed setbacks into shared experiences, fostering a sense of belonging and purpose. I learned that the journey from setback to success is rarely traveled alone, and that the power of community is the greatest asset in overcoming adversity.

VII. The Power of Community

Throughout my journey, community was the thread that held everything together. My family's unwavering support, the mentorship of leaders like Dr. Nicole and Sonji Grandy, and the encouragement of organizations like Dare to Dream Foundation, Profeta Foundation, and RU-Flourishing were instrumental in my transformation.

Among the most impactful mentors was Sonji Grandy, whose ongoing support over the following year helped me stay motivated in all areas. Sonji's approach was distinctive—her weekly calls created a space to review and reflect on my progress, and she encouraged me to pause and appreciate how far I had come rather than rush from one milestone to another. This outlook was invaluable, helping me avoid burnout and recognize my growth. With Sonji's guidance, I achieved sustainable success, balancing ambition with gratitude and self-care.

Community is more than a network—it is a source of strength, inspiration, and accountability. It provides the resources and relationships needed to overcome adversity and achieve greatness. In moments of doubt, the community lifts us up; in moments of triumph, it celebrates with us.

VIII. Conclusion: Daring to Dream Together

My story is one of redemption, resilience, and the relentless pursuit of dreams. From the shadows of incarceration to the light of entrepreneurship, I have learned that success is not a solitary endeavor. It is forged in the crucible of community, shaped by the support and guidance of others.

To those who face obstacles, I offer this lesson: Dare to dream and surround yourself with people who believe in your potential. Invest in yourself, embrace education, and seek out mentors who can guide you. Build businesses, create art, and share your story. Most importantly, recognize that your journey is part of a larger tapestry—a community of dreamers, builders, and believers.

I am a work in progress, still climbing mountains and chasing dreams. I am not where I want to be, but I am far from where I used to be. My achievements are not mine alone—they are the product of a strong community that dared to dream with me.

THE WORK THAT OUTLIVES US

Sonji K. Grandy

If the beginning of this story was born in frustration, then its ending is rooted in redemption.

More than twenty-five years ago, four people sat in my living room asking a simple but dangerous question: *How can we serve people who are like us?* We did not yet know the ripple effects of that moment. We could not see the faces, the names, the futures that would one day be shaped by a single decision to stop complaining and start building. What we did know, even then, was that faith requires action. As Scripture reminds us, *"Faith by itself, if it is not accompanied by action, is dead"* (James 2:17).

This anthology stands as living proof that the work mattered.

The voices in these pages belong to returning citizens, men and women who have lived life on both sides of the prison walls and chose courage anyway. Their stories are not about erasing the past; they are about reclaiming the future. Through the Dare 2 Dream Institute, we did not offer perfection. We offered partnership and we offered accountability. We offered belief when belief felt out of reach. We trusted that transformation was possible because God specializes in making all things new (*2 Corinthians 5:17*).

This work was never carried out by one person alone.

Over the span of twenty-five years, Generation X Community Association has been stewarded by board members who gave their time, wisdom, and heart to a vision that often-required sacrifice without spotlight. Some served for seasons, others for decades, but all were foundational. Their leadership helped safeguard the mission, challenge the vision when necessary, and ensure that integrity, not convenience, guided our decisions.

To every board member who attended late-night meetings, wrestled through difficult choices, showed up when resources were scarce, and believed in people before outcomes were guaranteed, this legacy bears your fingerprints. Scripture tells us, *"Two are better than one, because they have a good return for their labor"* (Ecclesiastes 4:9). This organization stands because of collective labor rooted in shared purpose.

At the heart of that purpose has always been mentorship and ministry.

Community work is sacred ground to me. It has always been that way. It is not separate from my faith, it is an extension of it, a living expression of what I believe about God, people, and purpose. I have never been able to separate spirituality from service, because Scripture never intended for them to be divided. Faith was never meant to be confined to sanctuaries or reserved for Sundays. Ministry happens in real time, in real lives, in real struggle.

Ministry lives in how we show up for one another when no one is watching. It lives in consistency, accountability, and compassion. It lives in the quiet moments when someone feels unseen and chooses not to give up because another person chose to stand with them. Jesus did not build community from a distance, He walked with people, ate with them, challenged them, restored them, and believed in them before they believed in themselves. That model has always shaped how I lead and serve.

Mentorship, to me, is one of the most sacred forms of ministry.

It is not about authority or hierarchy, it is about presence. It is about walking alongside someone as they unlearn shame and relearn their worth. It requires listening more than speaking, patience more than judgment, and truth delivered with love. In the space of mentorship, people are not rushed to become something impressive; they are invited to become whole.

The Scripture tells us that *"iron sharpens iron"* (Proverbs 27:17), and I have seen that sharpening take place in real and sometimes uncomfortable ways.

Growth often comes through challenge, through honest reflection, and through relationships that refuse to allow stagnation. Mentorship is mutual, it strengthens both the mentor and the mentee. I have been sharpened by the very people I was called to serve, learning humility, resilience, and grace through their journeys.

In community work, especially with returning citizens, mentorship becomes a lifeline. Many are navigating life with wounds that are invisible but deeply felt, carrying rejection, fear, and uncertainty into spaces that are not always forgiving. To walk with them is to say, *You are not alone. Your past does not cancel your purpose. Your future is still unfolding.*

This is why the work matters. This is why it is sacred. Because every conversation, every second chance, every moment of belief becomes an act of ministry. It is faith with sleeves rolled up. It is love in motion. And it is how legacies rooted in grace are built, one life, one relationship, one act of obedience at a time.

In the space of returning citizens, mentorship becomes both refuge and responsibility. These individuals are often reintroduced to society carrying labels heavier than their dreams. But we chose to see them through a different lens, one shaped by grace and accountability. We believed what Scripture affirms: *"There is therefore now no condemnation for those who are in Christ Jesus"* (Romans 8:1). While society may keep score, faith calls us to restoration.

There were seasons when the work felt overwhelming, seasons that tested not just our capacity, but our conviction. Progress moved slowly, if it moved at all. Funding was uncertain, resources stretched thin, and outcomes were often unseen. There were moments when the vision felt heavier than the hands carrying it, when the work demanded more than we had to give and offered little reassurance in return.

These were the seasons no one applauded, the seasons of quiet persistence, where obedience mattered more than visibility and faith had to carry the work when recognition did not. They were marked by showing up without guarantees and trusting the purpose even when progress was hard to measure. We had to continue forward simply because the calling remained clear.

In those moments, resilience was not built through confidence, it was built through remembrance. We had to remember ***why*** we started. We had to remember who the work was for. And most importantly, we had to remember that we were never laboring alone. Even when support felt distant and answers delayed, faith reminded us that purpose is sustained by something greater than human strength.

Scripture became both anchor and compass: *"Let us not grow weary in doing good, for at the proper time we will reap a harvest if we do not give up"* (Galatians 6:9). That promise was not a slogan, it was survival. It carried us through moments when the math didn't make sense, when exhaustion whispered quit, and when doubt tried to redefine the calling.

We learned that weariness is not failure, it is evidence of effort. And giving up was never an option, because too many lives were attached to the work. Too many people were counting on consistency when circumstances were unpredictable. So, we kept showing up. We kept believing. We kept sowing seeds in faith, trusting that God would handle the growth.

It speaks through restored lives and reclaimed purpose, through returning citizens who now lead, mentor, and build with confidence, and through communities strengthened because someone, somewhere, refused to quit when quitting would have been easier.

What was once unseen is now undeniable. What was once planted in tears has grown into testimony. The harvest is not just measured in programs or numbers, it is measured in people who dared to hope again. And it stands as proof that faithful labor, even in the hardest seasons, is never wasted.

Today, the harvest speaks for itself.

The returning citizens whose voices fill this anthology are no longer defined by confinement. They are mentors, leaders, parents, professionals, and advocates. Their success is not accidental, it is the result of community investment, faith in action, and a refusal to discard human potential.

As a founder and Vice President of Generation X, I have come to understand that legacy is not about permanence, it is about continuity. It is about building something strong enough to outlive you and flexible enough to evolve. Legacy is measured by the lives that continue the work long after your voice grows quiet.

Generation X Community Association was never meant to be a monument. It was meant to be a movement. It is a movement carried by board members who governed with integrity, by mentors who poured out wisdom without expectation of recognition, by returning citizens who dared to dream again despite the odds, and by communities that refused to give up on their own even when doing so would have been easier.

And so, as this chapter closes, the mission remains open. The legacy lives in every life restored, in every hand extended instead of turned away, and in every act of faith that chose action over apathy when indifference would have been easier.

"Being confident of this, that He who began a good work in you will carry it on to completion" (Philippians 1:6).

This is the work.
This is the faith.
This is the legacy.

And it is still being written.

LEGACY IN MOTION

The Power of Community to Carry the Work Forward

Dr. Nicole B. Simpson

Legacy is not an object, a title, or a moment frozen in time. It is movement. It is what continues long after the original hands grow tired. It is the living evidence that pain was not wasted, that service mattered, and that community transformed struggle into shared strength.

This book was never meant to center a single person or organization. It exists to amplify voices that are often dismissed, minimized, or ignored—people whose stories are complex, unfinished, and worthy of dignity. These are stories of individuals who were told, explicitly or implicitly, that their worst moment defined them. Yet through community, compassion, and opportunity, they discovered something far more powerful: **their humanity was never lost**.

Specific Achievements: Proof That Change Is Possible

The work chronicled in these pages demonstrates that transformation does not require perfection—only access, belief, and consistency. Through Generation X Community Association and later the Dare 2 Dream Institute, service evolved from informal acts of care into intentional systems of empowerment.

What began as media advocacy and community engagement expanded into tangible outcomes:

- Families were supported during seasons of financial strain without humiliation.
- Youth in underserved school districts were introduced to financial literacy as a tool for agency, not privilege.
- Incarcerated men and women were offered something rare inside correctional walls: **hope without judgment**.

- Returning citizens were given an alternative to underemployment—the opportunity to imagine themselves as entrepreneurs, leaders, and contributors.

Books were placed into prison libraries. Curriculum was built from lived experience, not theory. Faith was shared without coercion. Education was offered without shame. Businesses were imagined by people who had never been encouraged to dream beyond survival.

These achievements were not the result of funding alone or flawless planning. They were the product of **showing up consistently**, even when the work was uncomfortable, emotionally taxing, or misunderstood.

Lessons Learned: Service Requires Humility, Boundaries, and Growth

One of the most profound lessons revealed through this journey is that **good intentions are not enough**. Delivery matters. Structure matters. Sustainability matters.

Service, when rooted in unresolved pain, can quietly become self-sacrifice without boundaries. The work taught that helping others preserve dignity requires first believing that dignity belongs to everyone—including the servant. Over time, boundaries became as important as generosity. Rest became as sacred as labor. Listening became more powerful than fixing.

Another critical lesson is that trauma does not disappear simply because time passes. Whether experienced through incarceration, economic loss, systemic injustice, or personal tragedy, trauma demands acknowledgment. Healing is not linear, and progress cannot be rushed.

Perhaps most importantly, the work reinforced this truth: **people do not need to be rescued—they need to be respected**. When individuals are trusted with responsibility, education, and opportunity, they often exceed expectations that were never placed on them before.

The Impact of Community: Where Individual Strength Becomes Collective Power

Community is the throughline of every chapter in this book. Not the romanticized version of community, but the real one—messy, demanding, and deeply human.

Community is the colleague who encourages you to ask for help when pride says stay silent.
Community is the incarcerated woman who dares to believe her life still holds value.
Community is the volunteer who walks through prison gates when others will not.
Community is the returning citizen who chooses collaboration over isolation.

It was the community that transformed humiliation into a mission. A community that turned survival into service. A community that reminded each person involved that no one heals alone.

Inside prisons, community looked like shared meals, honest conversations, and the courage to imagine life beyond concrete walls. Outside, it became mentorship, accountability, and partnership. Across generations, it became the passing down of wisdom earned the hard way.

Community did not erase injustice—but it provided a place to stand while confronting it.

Legacy Forward: Carrying the Work Beyond These Pages

This story does not end with a ribbon-cutting, a final program, or a completed book. Legacy lives in what continues.

It lives in the returning citizen who chooses entrepreneurship over despair.
It lives in the parent who can breathe easier during the holidays.
It lives in the student who now understands money as a tool, not a mystery.

It lives in the person who was once counted out and now mentors someone else.

The charge moving forward is not to replicate personalities, but to replicate **principles**:

- Serve without stripping dignity.
- Build systems that acknowledge trauma.
- Replace judgment with accountability.
- Choose collaboration over control.
- Believe that redemption is not theoretical—it is practical.

This work belongs to the community now. It always did.

Final Reflection

Legacy is not about being remembered—it is about being **multiplied**. It is about creating spaces where others can step fully into who they are becoming. It is about leaving behind tools instead of trophies, pathways instead of pedestals.

If these stories have done their work, they will not simply be read—they will be carried. They will inspire someone to show up differently, serve more compassionately, and believe more boldly in the possibility of transformation.

This is not the end.

This is the continuation.

This is their story.
And now, it becomes yours.

THE HARBINGERS OF LIGHT

DR. NICOLE B. SIMPSON, CFP®

Reverend Dr. Nicole B. Simpson, CFP®, is a practitioner with over 30 years of experience in the securities industry, which she entered in 1991, and holds Series 7, 63, and 65 Securities licenses. On September 11, 2001, her life was drastically changed as a financial planner working at 2 World Trade Center on the 73rd floor. Simpson was still in the building on the 44th floor when Tower 2 was hit during the attacks on the World Trade Center. Today, Simpson compassionately helps families begin their journey toward recovery when faced with a catastrophic, unexpected disaster. She is actively involved in spiritual, emotional, and economic empowerment. As a compelling speaker on empowerment, a television and radio personality, and an author, Ms. Simpson travels across the United States teaching in a practical and easy-to-understand manner. Her simple approach encourages everyone who hears her message to take action and change their future. Her focus is to inspire people with the question, "If money were not an issue, what would be your life's purpose?"

Pastor Nicole's life began to take shape when she turned 7. Gifted with a Bible by her mom, she spent most of her time in her room reading the red words, which sparked her interest. Those red words told her to do good to please God and taught her how to pray. It was through Scripture that she learned how to seek God's comfort in the midst of every storm. Like most individuals, she has suffered an unexpected, significant personal tragedy that affected her entire family emotionally and financially. What is critical, but often avoided, is the experience and willingness to share strategies that instruct others on how to overcome unexpected disasters that can stagnate one's personal life because of a crisis. "How does one pick up the pieces of their life and move toward their ordained purpose?" She can answer those questions and put the necessary steps for beginning the recovery process into perspective.

In January 2016, she started a new chapter in her life by becoming the Pastor of Micah 7 Ministries in Piscataway, NJ. Her media appearances include TEDxMaviliSquare in May 2023, ABC News, CNN, BBC World News,

Huffington Post, Crain's NY Business, Fox News, PBS, and UPN 9. She serves as a Board Member of the CFP Board Center for Financial Planning Diversity Advisory Group, Chair of the Generation X Community Association, and Provost of the Dare 2 Dream Institute. She frequently speaks on the lecture circuit and has written several books on financial and life planning. Two of her books, Dare 2 Dream and The Quiet Shift, received third place in the BookFest Awards and were featured on the NASDAQ billboard in Times Square. Additionally, The Quiet Shift was a 2023 International Book Award Finalist in the Health: Aging/50+ category and won the inaugural Literary Global Book Award in the same category. Her dedication to financial education and planning earned her spots on Investopedia's Top 100 Independent Financial Advisors for 2022 and 2023, Investment News Hot 100 for 2023, and recognition as a Woman to Watch Trailblazer of the Year Finalist, as well as an honorable mention as Trailblazer of the Year by Invest in Others in 2023. In November 2023, she released her strategic leadership guidebook, Out of the Woods, Put Some Respect on Our Names, with her sister. In December 2023, she again appeared on the Times Square billboard for her numerous accomplishments.

Her latest book, Breaking Free From Financial Trauma, quickly became an Amazon bestseller upon its September 2024 release. In December 2024, Dr. Simpson was named Thought Leader of the Year at the Luminaries Awards and received the MYCPE ONE Excellence Award as a Mover and Shaker in the accounting industry. She earned a Doctorate in Transformational Leadership with top honors from Boston University, a Master of Divinity (Magna Cum Laude) from New Brunswick Theological Seminary, and a Bachelor of Science (Cum Laude) from Oral Roberts University. After 35 years of industry experience, recognizing that an economic and cultural reckoning is underway, Simpson is equipped to realize she is an anomaly and has much to contribute to the inevitable change America is demanding. This reality demands that she be available as a "teacher, trainer, mentor, guidance counselor."

SONJI K. GRANDY

Sonji K. Grandy has spent more than 30 years in the insurance industry, specializing in serving affluent clients and helping families protect their assets through thoughtful and strategic risk management. Her dedication to excellence and service has earned her national recognition, including being named one of Insurance Business America's Elite Women of the Year in 2021 and 2022 for her exceptional value through white-glove service, advocacy, and commitment to others. She was also recognized on Insurance Business America's Hot 100 list in 2022 and 2023, highlighting her outstanding contributions to the insurance industry.

Sonji is also a 17-time award-winning author of four books, whose work has received international recognition across multiple literary platforms. Her debut book, Beautifully Blended, received a BookFest Honorable Mention, was a finalist for a Literary Global Award, and earned an International Impact Award. Her second book, Mentoring With Confidence, earned First Place Honors from The BookFest Awards and The International Impact Awards. Her third book, Out of the Woods, received Second Place Honors and top recognition from the International Impact Awards. Her fourth book, Through Our Eyes, co-authored with her daughter, further reflects her passion for storytelling, mentorship, and generational healing.

Her literary work has been recognized in categories including Parenting & Family, Motivational, Women in Business, Business Leadership, Professional Growth, and Sustainable Business Practices. These accomplishments led to Sonji being featured on the Nasdaq Billboard in New York's Times Square, celebrating her impact as both an author and entrepreneur.

In addition to her professional and literary achievements, Sonji is a passionate advocate for Diversity, Equity, and Inclusion (DEI) initiatives. She focuses on uplifting marginalized and often overlooked communities of color within the insurance industry and beyond.

Sonji is the CEO and Founder of Sonji K Grandy Consulting, LLC, where she provides mentorship, leadership development, and guidance to emerging leaders. Through her work, she helps individuals navigate challenges, make informed decisions, and develop the confidence and skills needed to thrive professionally and personally.

She also serves as the Vice President of Generation X Community Association, a nonprofit organization dedicated to investing time, talent, and resources to support youth, underserved populations, and individuals who have experienced incarceration throughout New Jersey. The organization believes that faith, resilience, and community support can empower individuals to overcome trauma and rebuild their lives.

During the pandemic in 2020, Sonji continued her mission of service by launching the online blog www.itsabattle.com, a safe space where individuals could share experiences and find encouragement during an uncertain time.

A Minister, mentor, author, and community advocate, Sonji remains committed to building safe spaces where people can grow, heal, and discover their purpose. She balances her professional work, ministry, and community service with dedication and grace.

Sonji is a devoted wife, mother, and woman of strong faith, continuing to inspire others through her leadership, storytelling, and commitment to empowering the next generation.

VINCENT MCDONALD

Vincent McDonald is an entrepreneur, author, and podcast host whose life reflects resilience, faith, and transformation. Raised in New Jersey, he turned a fifteen-year prison sentence into a period of profound growth, earning multiple certificates and degrees while incarcerated. After his release, he pursued business studies, launched ventures in publishing and property management, and became an advocate for formerly incarcerated entrepreneurs. Through storytelling, mentorship, and community building, Vincent inspires others to turn setbacks into purpose and lasting impact.

MICHAEL MIDDLETON

Michael Middleton is a redemption-driven author, entrepreneur, and visionary committed to transforming lived experience into legacy. After overcoming incarceration, he rebuilt his life through discipline, self-awareness, and faith, channeling adversity into purpose-driven leadership. Founder of Michael Middleton Consulting LLC and creator of the A+ Vision Is Power (VIP) brand, Michael develops impactful adult and children's works that inspire growth, imagination, and generational change, with new releases slated for 2026.

SHAVON PRICE

Shavon Price is a solution-driven multi-potentialite with a thirst for time management. Having spent a decade honing her skills in complex project planning within Fortune 40 companies, Shavon knew the ins and outs of operational strategies like no other. Her well-rounded experience in corporate event and travel planning, customer relations, and document management sets her apart from the crowd.

In 2020, Shavon took a leap of faith and founded She's Your Assistant. This virtual assistant agency was not just another run-of-the-mill service; it was a game-changer. It gave her the freedom to earn and learn on the go. With a mission to give entrepreneurs back their most precious resource - time - Shavon understood that to truly help entrepreneurs scale their businesses, she needed to harness the power of AI and process automation.

Her passion for time management comes from her eagerness to embark on new experiences

AYESHA ROGERS

Ayesha Rogers works for Newark Community Street Team, which partners with the University Hospital Violence Intervention Program. She works alongside individuals and families impacted by violence as they reclaim safety, dignity, and hope. Grounded in empathy and trust, she uses a trauma - informed approach to help people heal, access critical resources, and rebuild their lives without fear of re-victimization. She is known for meeting people where they are. She is deeply committed to helping others move forward with strength- no longer having to look over their shoulders.

TIYANNA SCARLETT

Tiyanna Scarlett is a woman of faith, resilience, and purpose whose life reflects the redemptive power of God's grace and education. After beginning her journey as an incarcerated student in 2010, she earned her bachelor's and master's degrees in social work from Rutgers University. She now serves as an Academic Counselor at East Jersey State Prison and has years of experience as a drug and alcohol counselor supporting individuals facing addiction, trauma, and mental health challenges.

As the founder and proud owner of ReNewHer, a faith-centered initiative committed to supporting women impacted by incarceration, addiction, trauma, and mental health, Tiyanna is committed to helping them reclaim their identity, rebuild their lives, rediscover their worth, and walk boldly in purpose. Tiyanna uses her voice to testify to the power of redemption, restoration, and second chances. Her story stands as living proof that incarceration does not define destiny and that through faith, education, and purpose, transformation is always possible.

FAWN STRATTON

Fawn Renee Stratton is a faith-driven entrepreneur, advocate, and powerful voice for transformation. Born and raised in Asbury Park, New Jersey, she overcame childhood abuse, foster care, addiction, incarceration, and a colon cancer diagnosis to rebuild her life with purpose and determination. Becoming a mother at 18 only strengthened her resolve to create a better future.

Today, Fawn is the founder of a successful credit repair business dedicated to helping others restore their financial standing and reclaim their confidence. A college graduate honored with multiple awards, she uses both her professional expertise and lived experience to inspire change in the lives of others.

Her mission is to open sober living homes and build generational wealth for her family while continuing to uplift those facing the struggles she once endured. Through faith, resilience, and relentless perseverance, Fawn Renee Stratton proves that your past does not define your future.

DAMON VENABLE

Damon Venable is a *Community Engagement Specialist and Paralegal.* A graduate of the Rutgers School of Criminal Justice, he has more than thirty years of paralegal experience. Since returning home in 2021, Damon has been exemplifying his transformation and lived experience in the capacity of an effective community advocate, community defender, reentry consultant, motivational speaker, and mentor. Damon currently serves as the Vice-Chairman of the NJDOC Board of Trustees for the Adult Facilities. He is also the author of his memoir-biography, *A Beautiful Pain.*

JASMINE WILKES

Jasmine Wilkes is married with two sons. She lives in South Jersey with her beautiful family and is now a proud homeowner. By profession, she works as a medical billing representative for Pharmaceutical and Tactical Healthcare Services. Jasmine's education includes a phlebotomy certification, a diploma in medical billing and coding, and an associate degree in Health Information Technology. She is currently enrolled at DeVry University, where she is diligently working toward earning her Bachelor of Science degree in Health Information Management, with a planned graduation date in 2027. She published her first book, "Fears, Tears & Years," in 2018 with Harvest Wealth Publishing and has since contributed to the book "In and of the World Again" for Newark's returning citizens support group.

Since then, Jasmine has used her voice as an empowerment speaker to share her story of overcoming oppression and to highlight issues within the justice system, continuing to advocate for those still incarcerated. She has been featured as both a speaker and a keynote at various organizations and events. Jasmine is a proud member of Micah 7 Ministries in Plainfield, New Jersey, under the leadership of Rev. Dr. Nicole B. Simpson and Rev. Dr. Angel Thompson. She is also affiliated with the Generation X Organization and the SPEAR group at The College of New Jersey (TCNJ), where she annually serves as a keynote speaker for the freshman English literature class.

From the Publisher

ARE EVEN BETTER WHEN THEY'RE SHARED!

HELP OTHER READERS FIND THIS ONE:

- Post reviews at your favorite online booksellers
- Post a picture on your social media accounts and share why you enjoyed it
- Send a note to a friend or colleague who would also love it-or better yet, gift them a copy!

Thanks for reading!

www.ingramcontent.com/pod-product-compliance
Lightning Source LLC
LaVergne TN
LVHW020511100826
845148LV00003B/752

* 9 7 9 8 9 8 7 1 7 8 2 9 4 *